Cyril's Cake Adventure

Because every cake
has a story to tell

Projects

Forword

I first met Rhianydd around 15 years ago, when I was working for Cake Decoration and Sugarcraft magazine. Even then Rhi stood out amongst all the other cake artists as being quite special. Her designs, although Rhi disagrees with me, were quite different from the usual wedding cakes around at the time.

Rhi developed her own unique style and her role as a Cake International judge, her show features, demonstrations and workshops prove what a very talented lady she is.

I am extremely honoured to write the foreword for Rhianydd's very first book, and, if you are looking for a tool to enhance your creativity, look no further as this is an escapism into the magical mind of Rhianydd Webb.

Melanie Underwood

House Brownie created with the kind permission of Tony Di'Terlizzi for Cake International magazine and the Spiderwick Fieldguide feature at Cake International March 2017

About the Book

Every cake has a story to tell, so why not a tutorial book with a children's story.

Each chapter page is the next page of the story, which I hope you will read with your nearest and dearest and share the projects and recipes with them in the same way that my boys did with the cake books on my shelves.

If the book gets a little bit messy, all the better.
There is nothing worse than an unused book.

I began my cake business so that I could work from home and be there for my children as they grew up. They went everywhere with me, which created so many memories because we spent so much time together, and that, I treasure.

They are now 24 and 21 and wonderful kind men.
Over the years, they spent many hours in the three cake shops I have had (don't worry, they usually had their own space there and even asked for jobs); they have been to all of the wedding venues in South Wales and beyond, and attended numerous cake shows, particularly the Squires Kitchen exhibition, which was their home each year.

They treasure having been helpers to the wonderful Sir Eddie Spence MBE, watched fabulous demonstrations by cake, chocolate, isomalt and cookery masters and I believe the experiences helped shape them into the wonderful men they are today.

My boys pored through all my treasured cake decorating books and were inspired to create their own cakes, so I wanted to create a book that other children would be drawn to.

Hopefully, the projects in this book will inspire the children in your lives to share the wonderful journey that my boys and I have taken over the years.

Maybe to make cakes for their own family and friends, or even to go to a cake show or compete!

I do hope you enjoy the book, and if you create something from there, please do pop by my facebook page and share pictures.

If you need clarification for any of the projects in the book, please get in touch via my Dragons and Daffodils Cakes facebook page. I can't promise that I can reply instantly, but I will reply.

Skills Index

Rather than put all the skills in the front of the book, the skills are throughout the book.

There are projects from simple cupcakes through to sculpted cakes with internal armatures.

So if you want to know how to cover a cake, or wire a leaf, simply look it up in the skills index and go straight to that page.

I have tried to include multiple methods for certain skills such as wiring leaves or petals as I don't believe that everyone works the same way.

Dessert Table

The book was designed so that you could make:

- the smaller projects from each chapter
- or the finished project
- or if you create everything, make a complete display

Complimentary Products

I wanted to design a range of products that would help not only the beginner, but the commercial cake business.
So there are stencils, Sugar Press embossers, a mould and cookie cutters. I wanted these products to enable those that felt they couldn't draw or model or paint, to see that we all can. We just need a little encouragement.

Thank you to Vanilla Valley, Sugar Press by Crafty Designs and FPC Sugarcraft for their help to create these.

Chapters

Hello

I am so pleased that you found this book.
There is a special story in here just for you.
Just make sure you help the adults make the cakes too,
they need your help.
Happy Caking.

Rhi

Skills

Recipes

1

The Pawprint

"What is it!" said Cyril the squirrel, scratching his lovely and tufty chestnut ear.

He leaned over the strange and new paw print.

"I've never seen anything like this before."

SNIFF SNIFF!

"What is it!"

Cyril was all grown-up. Well…… nearly………
He had lived in the woods for eight moons now,
he didn't need to see one more moon to be grown-up?…………surely!

He looked UP   UP   UP

high up through the trees to the shiny golden sun in the sky.

"hmm" thought Cyril "the sun is sliding lower and lower towards the trees.
It will soon be night-time."

"I must tell Olly the owl, he will know what to do!"

And off he scampered to the great old tree.

Cookies

Cookies can be very simple or very detailed.
They are perfect for all levels and all ages.
Replace the flavouring with your favourite or experiment and create your own.

Ingredients

- 200G block stork
- 200g caster sugar
- 400g plain flour
- 2oz or 1 large eggs
- 1 tsp vanilla extract
- 1 tbsp cocoa powder

Equipment

- Baking tray
- Silicone mat
- Mixer
- Large bowl
- Rolling pin
- Cookie cutters by Rhianydd Webb: squirrel, paw print, tree.

Method

- Cream butter and sugar until pale
- Beat eggs with vanilla and add with flour to the creamed mix until combined.
- Lightly knead
- Divide in two and add cocoa powder to one batch
- Refrigerate for 1 hour
- Roll out gently on floured surface to 3-5mm thick depending on the size of the biscuit. (Larger biscuit may need to be thicker to avoid breakages).
- Cut out the shapes and carefully remove the excess dough.
- Re-roll only once and refrigerate after re-rolling.
- Place cut out biscuits in the fridge until cold.
- Bake for 8-12 (or 12-16) minutes at 160 degrees C
- Take out after the edges turn brown but are still pale in the centre
- Cool on the tray which then helps it crisp

Pawprint Cookie

Ingredients

- 180g chocolate cookie dough
- Magic Colours dark brown and black airbrush colour

Equipment

- Nail brush
- Rolling pin
- Sugarpress pawprint embosser
- Baking tray
- Silicone mat
- Clairella Cakes airbrush

**Want a shaped cookie instead?
Why not texture the dough with the nail brush,
then simply cut out a pawprint cookie cutter shape**

Large shaped and textured cookies are so much more fun than a small cookie.

And who doesn't love extra cookies.

Roll out 180g of chocolate cookie dough to 5mm thick.
Texture with a nail brush and push in the sugarpress cat pawprint embosser. Rip the edges to make it uneven. Bake for 15 minutes and cool on the tray.

Airbrush in the pawprints with black and airbrush the rest of the cookie with a mix of kroma brown and magic colours dark brown.

Tree Cookies

Ingredients

- 170g chocolate cookie dough
- Magic colour airbrush colour: dark brown and black
- 20g vanilla cookie dough
- Sugarflair spruce green gel colour
- 15g Renshaws chocolate brown sugarpaste
- Piping gel
- Squires Kitchen bulrush dust colour
- Rainbow Dust holly green gel colour
- Coconut

Equipment

- Baking tray
- Silicone mat
- Small rolling pin
- FPC Sugarcraft bark mat
- Clairella Cakes Airbrush
- Rhianydd Webb tree cookie cutter
- Pastry brush
- SK palette knife
- SK dresden

Baking a Shaped Tree Trunk Cookie

There are so many possibilities with cookies.

They don't all have to be flat. Whole scenes can be created by baking the dough over foil shapes, or by shaping smaller pieces before baking.

Have fun experimenting.

Roll out the chocolate cookie dough to 5mm thick and measuring 10cm x 15cm.
Press onto the FPC Sugarcraft bark mat and push the paste into all the indentations.

Prepare a foil support as in the picture and roll the cookie dough around the foil with the pattern face up. Add a small piece of cookie dough to the side of the trunk as in the next image. Place the Cookie on a silicone mat to cook for 18 minutes then remove the support and bake for a further 15 minutes. Cool on the tray

Airbrush inside the trunk hollow and along the lines with Magic Colours dark brown.

Airbrush further with black to emphasise.

Roll out 20g of spare biscuit dough coloured with Sugarflair spruce green and back for 8 minutes. Allow to cool. Break down to crumbs and re-bake for 8 more minutes until it begins to turn brown. Cool, then break to small crumbs in a sandwich bag.

Colour a small amount of royal icing (recipe p.14) with SK bulrush dust colour. Half fill a piping bag by picking up the royal icing on the palette knife, slide into the bottom of the piping bag, grip the bag between finger and thumb and slide the knife out leaving the royal icing inside.

Fold the sides of the bag up and fold down the top until the folded bag is tight to the royal icing. Snip off the very tip to create a 2mm hole.
Pipe a small amount onto the log and sprinkle the green biscuit crumbs onto the royal icing.

Decorating Flat Tree Cookies

Using 15g brown sugarpaste, roll out a sausage of paste. Cut two slits at the top 1cm down and separate the sections. Fix on with piping gel.

Use the dresden to push and pull extra depth in such as squirrel holes.

Split dessicated coconut into two bowls and colour both with Rainbow dust holly/green food colouring, one lighter than the other. Mix them together.

Colour royal icing with Sugarflair spruce green and half fill a piping bag. Pipe onto the tree cookie.

Sprinkle the coloured coconut onto the royal icing.

Leave until set before gently shaking off the excess coconut.

Wear gloves when working with coloured coconut as the colour stains.

Royal Iced Squirrel Cookie

Ingredients

- Squires Kitchen royal icing mix made up to instructions
- Magic Colours airbrush colours: chestnut, dark brown
- Magic Colours Pro super white
- Rainbow Dust brown food colouring pen
- Culpitt dipping solution

Equipment

- PME parchment piping bags
- Piping tips - 1, 1.5, 2
- Detail brush
- Scissors
- No.6, 8 filbert brushes
- Palette
- Ramequin
- Squirrel cutter
- Scalpel
- PME scribe
- Tray & silicone mat

Royal icing is quite simple to make by beating 1 large egg white, then gradually beating in 250g of sifted icing sugar until it is glossy and forms soft peaks when a spoon dipped in the icing is lifted (ie the peak gently falls to the side rather than remaining upright which is firm peak). However, icing sugar is being produced differently now, so it is often clumpy and grainy.

For a smooth royal icing, I use Squires Kitchen royal icing mix as in the equipment picture.

I pipe with soft peak icing, so check the consistency with the spoon. If it is too loose, add a tablespoon of icing sugar and check again. If it is too firm, add a few drops of water until it reaches the required consistency.

Cookies are flooded in with flood icing which has been diluted with water (or you can use egg white for a stronger icing)

Trace the template onto greaseproof piper. Cut out the eyehole and use a scalpel to mark along the inner details. Transfer the pattern through the greaseproof paper using a food colour pen. Make SK soft peak royal icing by adding drops of water to the icing until when a spoon is dipped and lifted, the peak just falls over.

Colour 3/4 royal icing with berberis dust.

Piping bags

Place a parchment triangle with the horizontal side on the top. Coil the left point clockwise and hold in place with your left hand. Wrap the right point around the main section and ensure both points are down and straight.

Cut half the length of a piping tip off the end of the bag, insert the tip and gently pull into place, then half fill the bag by sliding a palette knife loaded with royal icing into the bag and squeezing the bag to hold the icing inside and slide the knife out. Fold the sides of the bag up then roll or fold the top down to seal.

The PME scribe is great to swirl the icing into place and pop bubbles.

Half fill a bag with white soft peak royal icing (no tip). Pipe a white line around the muzzle, chest and belly, touching the bag to the cookie, squeeze at the same time as lifting, stop squeezing just before you want to stop, drop the line into place and touch the bag to the cookie to stop the line. Fill the shapes and neaten by swirling a scribe in the icing, moving it to

the template line.
Half fill a bag with berberis flood icing and a no.2 tip. Fill the top right ear in the same way with berberis flood icing and also the far right paw. Pipe the outline for the tail with another bag with a no. 1.5 tip filled with berberis soft peak icing.

Fill the tail with berberis flood icing, taking care that there is enough royal icing in the area so that the tail doesn't look hollow when it settles.

For flood icing, dilute soft peak royal icing with a few drops of water so that when stirred, the trail takes 10 seconds to smooth back out.

Use the soft peak icing and a no.2 tip to pipe the outline for the body.
Pipe a line around the eye which will become the upper and lower eye lids. Dry for 20 minutes under a spotlight so that the icing doesn't merge together.

Flood the body area by starting to pipe just inside the line at the back, and piping side to side filling the area. Work across the shape taking care not to leave too long between piping a section and flooding it as it will be difficult to blend.

Place the piped cookie under a spotlight for a few more minutes before piping the legs and face in the same way so that the icing sections next to each other don't bleed into each other, but keep distinct raised and curved edges to the section.

After a few more minutes under the lamp, pipe around the ear in the foreground. You can also pipe a little more white onto the upper jaw area to make it more prominent. Leave under the lamp for 10 minutes then leave in a cardboard box overnight to dry.

Airbrush Magic Colours chestnut colour along the back, down the tail, legs, cheek and down the snout. Mix equal drops of Magic Colours chestnut and dark brown together and airbrush the base of the feet. Leave the white areas untouched for now, but we will dirty him up a little later.

Airbrush Magic Colours dark brown over the joints of the legs, colour most of the tail, along the back, behind the neck and the feet, emphasising the shadows..
Paint the dark brown colour to define the edge of the ear, nose and the opening of the mouth. Paint a white dot for the eye.

Rock and Shrub Cookies

Ingredients

- Royal icing
- Green cookie crumbs
- Sugarflair spruce green colour
- 80g vanilla cookie dough
- Kroma black and green airbrush colours

Equipment

- Pawprint cookie cutter
- Sharp knife
- Silicone mat
- Baking tray
- Parchment piping bag
- Palette knife
- Scissors
- Rhianydd Webb Pawprint cookie cutter
- Nailbrush
- Aluminium foil
- Rolling Pin

Even the simplest shaped cookies make a scene look really interesting.

Try experimenting with texture as well as shape but remember, the deeper the cookie, the longer it will need to bake.

To stop burning, cover with foil after 15 minutes in the oven.

Roll lumps of vanilla cookie dough into rough shapes betwen 13g and 32g each. Place on the silicone mat and press with scrunched up kitchen foil to texture. Bake for 12-15 minutes depending on size.

What else can you think of creating with this method?

Allow the cookies to completely cool. Airbrush lightly with kroma black sugarpaste. Swiping across the rock cookies in one direction to allow shading to occur naturally. Add more colour at the base.

Roll out green coloured cookie dough. Texture with a nailbrush. Cut out using the paw print cookie cutter. Use a knife to cut the base flat. Bake for 8-10 minutes. Cool on the silicone mat on a cooling rack. Airbrush Kroma green to shade.

Assembling the Scene

Ingredients

- Royal icing: chocolate brown
- Cookie crumbs: shades of green
- Piping gel
- 200g Renshaws chocolate brown sugarpaste
- Cookies & cookie supports

Equipment

- Palette knife and sharp knife
- 10" round cake drum
- 15mm brown satin ribbon
- Double sided tape
- Scissors
- Nailbrush
- PME scalpel

Cut small triangles of vanilla and chocolate cookie dough and bake for 8-10 minutes for the cookie supports.

Scrape the baked supports with a scalpel until they fit neatly against the cookies. Pipe a line of chocolate brown icing down the support and sit against the cookie.

Draw around the pawprint cookie to create a template. Fix the pawprint cooke to the front centre of the base board with the chocolate brown royal icing.

Knead 200g of Renshaws chocolate flavoured sugarpaste. Dust the work surface with icing sugar and roll out. Roll from the middle to the back and the middle to the front to thin quickly. Push a nailbrush into the paste to texture.

Moisten the cake board with water around the cookie. Place the pawprint cookie template onto the sugarpaste and cut to shape. Place onto the board and use the nailbrush to push the paste into place neatly around the cookie. Now for the fun bit.

Pipe chocolate brown royal icing onto the base of all the items and arrange them onto the board. The squirrel will sit on the pawprint cookie. Fit double sided tape around the board edge and add ribbon, starting at the back and stretching taught to wrap. Cut the end at an angle.

In the Woods

The great old tree was in the heart of the
Green Oak Woods.
It was a wonderful place to live, Swishy-wishy green
leaves danced high above your head.

Can you swish?

Each time the wind swished and swooshed.......whipped
and whooped through the trees, all the deliciously
crunchy leaves on the woodland floor twirled
gracefully in and out of the sparkling sunbeams.
Toasty and warm.

"There is the great old tree!" said Cyril

Can you spot the paw prints?

2

Lining a Cake Tin

If you have never baked before, lets go back to basics.
If you already bake, you can skip this bit.

Ingredients

- Butter or margarine

Equipment

- Greaseproof paper
- Scissors
- 7" round cake tin (mine is 4" tall but a sandwich tin is perfect)

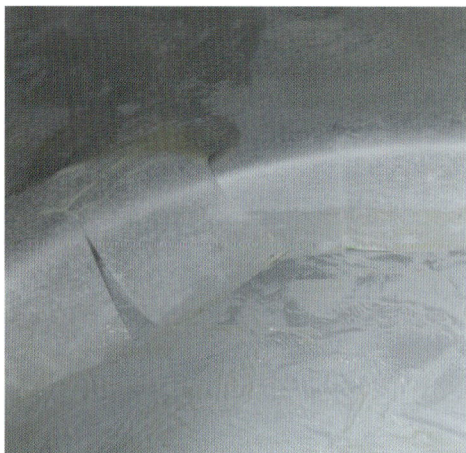

Place the cake tin on top of the greaseproof paper and draw around the tin with a non toxic pencil. Wrap greaseproof paper around the outside of the tin and cut a length one inch longer and one inch taller. Use scissors to cut a fringe into one side of the long strip of greaseproof paper.

Grease the inside walls and inside base of the tin using butter and a spare piece of greaseproof paper.

Wrap the side strip around the inside of the tin wall with the fringe at the bottom. Ensure the fringe is neatly in place on the bottom of the tin. Finally, place the cut out circle (with the pencil side down so it doesn't touch the cake batter) and smooth into place.

Lemon Buttercream

Ingredients

- 210g unsalted butter
- 300g sifted icing sugar
- 1tsp lemon extract

Method

1. Measure out the room temperature ingredients.
2. Beat the butter in the mixer until fluffy
3. Beat in the icing sugar and lemon extract for one minute.

Lemon Sponge Cake

This is a simple sponge recipe which you can either choose to cream the butter and sugar together as you do for a Victoria Sandwich, or use the all-in-on method. Both give you a deliciously light cake.
This is also a great recipe for cupcakes and will yield approximately 16.   Just bake for 10-15 mins at 180C fan/gas mark 4

Ingredients

- 500g caster sugar
- 500g Stork margarine or unsalted butter
- 500g egg without shell
- 500g McDougalls sponge flour
- 4tbsp milk (I used soy)
- Grated zest of 2 lemons and flavour to taste

Equipment

- Five 6" round sandwich tins greased and lined
- Large bowl
- Mixer or wooden spoon
- Bowls to pre-weigh ingredients
- Cake tester
- Oven gloves

Method

1. Weigh out all the ingredients.
2. Ensure they are all at room temperature before you begin and that you have sifted the flour.
3. **All in one method** - put all prepared ingredients into a bowl and beat until they are smooth and incorporated.
4. I used my Kenwood and a K-beater but you can use a wooden spoon or spatula.
5. Careful not to overbeat.
6. **Creaming method** - cream the butter and sugar together. Add the eggs one at a time with the addition of a tablespoon of flour to avoid curdling.
7. Finally, gently fold in the sieved flour

8. Bake in the centre of an oven preheated to 190C or 170C fan assisted or Gas mark 5.
9. Bake for 20-25 minutes or until the cake has slightly shrunk away from the sides, springs back to the touch and a cake tester or skewer comes out clear.
10. You can see my 4" tall tin here, but I like to bake in layers so a sandwich tin is good if you have them.

Turn out upside down on a cooling rack until cool.

The cooling rack pattern.

Alternative flavours:
Replace the lemon zest for :

- 1tsp of vanilla extract or bean paste
- 1 tsp
- Orange zest
- Chocolate chips

Ganache and Sharp Edges

Ganache can really help achieve good sharp edges on a sugarpasted cake.
The Ingredients for all three flavours are included and the method is the same for each.

Ingredients

Dark Ganache
- 300ml dcream
- 600g dark chocolate

Milk Ganache
- 300ml double cream
- 750g milk chocolate

White Ganache
- 300ml double cream
- 900g white chocolate
  (in the summer I use between 1050g-1200g of white chocolate to the same quantity of cream instead)

Which ganache you choose is totally up to you.

For wedding cakes I prefer to use white chocolate as the icing is usually pale, but dark chocolate is thc strongest.

Making Ganache Method

Please Note:

The cream is extremly hot

It can cause burns

Please use caution.

Weigh out the chocolate for your chosen ganache recipe. Chop up into 1cm pieces and place in a bowl.

Weigh cream and place in glass jug.

Microwave for 5 minutes until the cream reaches a rolling boil where the bubbling cream on the surface appears to roll over and over.

Quickly pour evenly over the room temperature chococolate. Leave the mixture without touching for two minutes.

Stir in a figure of eight motion to evenly blend the two ingredients until it resembles peanut butter consistency.
Straight away cling film the ganache so that the cling film covers both the inside of the bowl and the surface of the ganache.

Splitting and filling the cake.

Trim the tops off the layers so that they now measure 1 1/4" tall. Spread a little buttercream onto the 6" board and add the first layer

Spread 100g evenly on the cake layer. Place the cake on a scale and add 100g buttercream between each layer.

Wrap the cake in cling film and leave at room temperature to settle for four hours. This helps to avoid buttercream bulges once the bubbles have burst.

Use three food safe dowels and cut one to the height of the cake. Mark the other two and cut them the same. Sand the edges and wash before inserting evenly.

Check that there is a 4mm gap either side of the cake. If not, carve away neatly from top to bottom with a serrated carving knife. You can see the ganache plate with the gap here.

Ganaching the Cake

Ganache
Check the side is level before you add the ganache and trim further if it isn't.

Add a crumb coat to seal in the cake, paddle the ganache on to the cake by moving the palette knife side to side. The ganache will neaten any gaps.

Scrape firmly to remove ganache around the side until both ganache plates are visible. Leave overnight. Remove the top plate and the dowels.

Use a palette knife to paddle a 4mm thick layer on top with a palette knife. Rotate the cake and smooth with the palette knife to level the surface.

Use the scraper on the sides to remove the excess ganache from the top coat. I then add a thin layer to the side of the cake to neaten it.

Slice with a palette knife from the outer edge into the middle to neaten. Leave overnight to set, then neaten the cake with a hot dry knife.

Splitting and filling the cake.

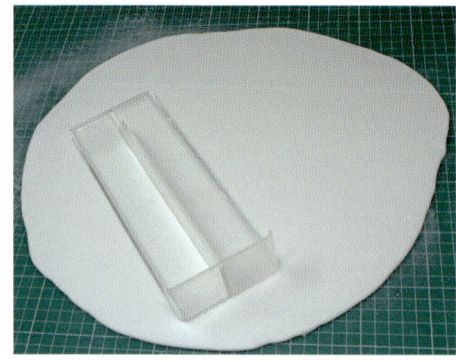

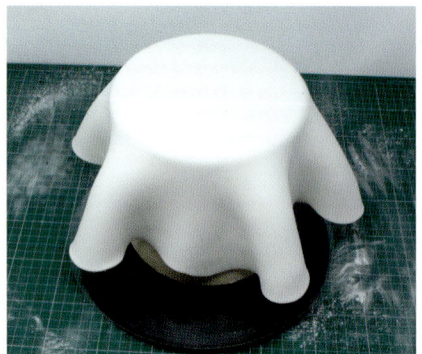

Sugarpaste

Always knead your sugarpaste before using to activate the gums. Press it firmly on a clean surface, push away from you to stretch, fold back and repeat. Knead only until the top surface is smooth, then dust the worktop with icing sugar to roll out. (Always use icing sugar, not corn flour as corn flour can cause fermentation).

Roll out the sugarpaste with your chosen rolling pin. Roll away from you twice, then slide the paste clockwise 45 degrees to spread the icing sugar around and repeat. Too much rolling will stick it to the work surface so keep it moving. Polish the surface with a smoother before you cover the cake as it is easier to start with a good surface.

Support either with your rolling pin, or slide both hands underneath, supporting the paste on the palms of your hands and gently lower onto the cake.

When rolling out, don't flip over your sugarpaste like pastry. Only roll out on one side.

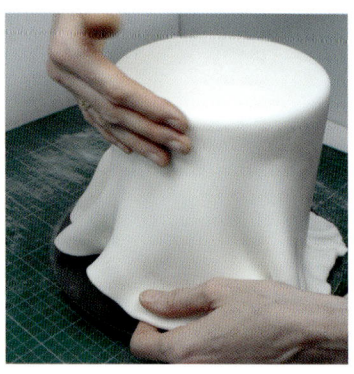

Rotate the smoother on the top and then stroke the paste onto the sides in an upward movement, (the royal wave) stretching out any creases by skirting as if straightening a table cloth.

If you need to stretch the paste, stroke the paste gently between finger and thumb, also use this method to remove a pleat.

Place a large acrylic disk on the top of the cake. Grip firmly with one hand on top and another underneath and turn the cake upside down by flipping quickly. Remove the base large disk and the ganaching plate.

Use the sharp edge smoother first by holding the bottom.
Smooth by moving from side to side about 2" at a time.
Work all the way around the cake, then move your hand up to the middle of the smoother to smooth the middle section, then repeat for the top.
Continue until the sides are neat and even.

Any blemishes can be neatened by polishing gently in a circular movement with the flexi smoother. The friction of the textured side will smooth the paste. To fix the edge, hold the smoothers as shown with one hand gently on top and both tightly together and move gently from side to side. Don't press hard to overly thin the paste.

Painting the Woodland scene

So many people tell me that they can't draw, so I designed this stencil especially for them.
Dusting on top of coconut oil gives a much richer finish to the colours and mistakes can easily be altered.

Ingredients
- Squires Kitchen cocoa butter
- Squires Kitchen dust colours: eidelweiss, sunflower, vine, leaf green, dark green, berberis, chestnut, bulrush, black, hydrangea
- Coconut Oil

Equipment
- The Vanilla Valley woodland stencils
- Brushes to include: 1/2" flat, no.8 filbert, Sugarpress brushes, fan brush
- Strong tape and greaseproof paper
- 20cm plate or metal palette and 1 pint bowl

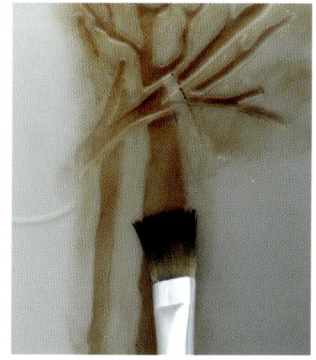
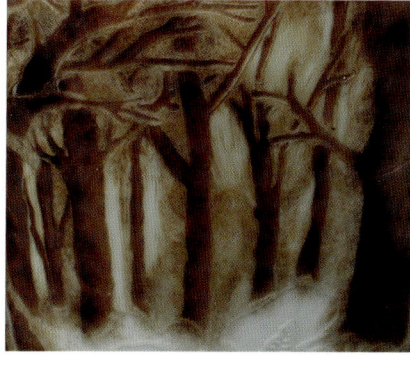

Fix strong tape onto the sides of the stencil. Grease the entire cake with coconut oil. Wrap greaseproof paper around the back of the cake, place the stencil in front, fixing to the greaseproof. Press with a smoother to fix.

(See P.26 for a photo of the stencil, tape and greaseproof).Dust chestnut onto all of the trees. Gently hold the sections of the stencil in place while you dust.

Complete the design, and add bulrush dust to the left hand side of the trees and the underside of branches to indicate shadows. Add patches onto the larger trees.

Dust the shrubs with vine green and the ferns with leaf green, stippling on the colour.

Use a fan brush and stipple extra colour onto the shrubs with vine green

Dust chestnut onto the fallen leaves.

Add depth around the edges of the shapes.

Remove the stencil carefully. Use a cotton bud to gently stroke away any blemishes.

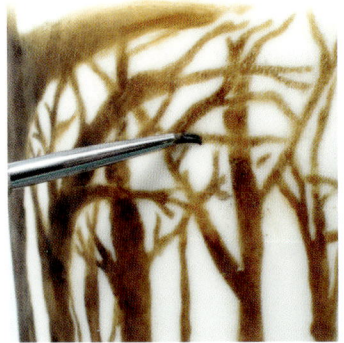

Use a Sugarpress brush to join the gaps in the tree branches, the dust will spread across, but to add colour, dust the same colours that you have already used.

Dust sunflower and vine lightly for the lower two thirds of the background between the trees. Dust hydrangea mixed with eidelweiss for the sky.

Dust a mix of berberis and chestnut over the fallen leaves. Darken with chestnut along the base of the shrubs.

Mix eidelweiss with black and lightly dust the path, stippling the colour on with a scruffy brush.

Darken the green in the lower background by mixing leaf green in with the vine and dusting the background. Dust the gaps between the shrubs with the same green.

Dust the lower background with a dark green mixed with leaf green.

Dust areas of the path first with black dust. Shake off the excess.
Lightly dust areas with bulrush. Aim for below the trees and in the distance.

Cocoa Butter Painting

Prepare the second stencil layer as described for the first layer (I thought it would be useful to show the greaseproof paper is on the left hand side and the stencil is laid on top (this protects the cake surface) and the tape is already attached to the greaseproof. Simply wrap around the cake and fix, it will stick to the coconut oil, so be gentle with this layer.

To melt the cocoa butter, Half fill a 1 pint bowl with boiling water. Sit a 20cm plate or aluminium palette on top of the bowl and add 2-3 callets of cocoa butter per colour you would like to use. I usually put a maximum of four areas of colour onto a plate to stop the colours from bleeding together. I also put an extra section of cocoa butter into the centre in case I need to dilute any colours further. If the colour becomes too runny when painting, remove the plate from on the bowl and allow it to cool.
I keep a thermos flask of hot water on my work space.
If you make a mistake, it can be removed with more cocoa butter, or scraped off.

Add vine green and eidelweiss to a little cocoa butter and stipple the colour on with a messy brush. Add leaf green to the mix and stipple again leaving gaps in the shape.

Mix leaf green with pure cocoa butter and stipple onto the edges. Mix eidelweiss with cocoa butter and use a clean brush to stipple the flower buds.

Using a small scruffy brush. Use the vine green and white cocoa butter mix and stipple the top of the shrubs. This also hides the stencil lines well.

Use a detail brush and leaf green mixed with cocoa butter to paint the edges of the leaves. Add extra to the base of the plant and depth to the shadows.

Use the vine green and white mix and a fine brush to paint a V shape on the underneath of the white flowers.

Dust the board first by stippling vine green, then over dust with leaf green.

Add chestnut and bulrush to darken some areas as on the cake. Dust a little berberis onto the darker areas to suggest at fallen leaves.

Mix bulrush and black with cocoa butter and paint to refine the darker edges of the trees. Also use black mixed with cocoa butter .

Use the bulrush and black to define the underneath of branches and to show where they cross each other.

Stand back and look at the scene to ensure that it has enough depth. Squint your eyes too so that you can see general shapes and colours easier.

Mix bulrush with cocoa butter and paint around the stencilled leaves to add definition to the woodland floor.

Complete the painting by adding freeform tiny leaf shapes trailing away from the stencilled leaf sections using vine and eidelweiss mix and leaf green and vine mix.

Honey Cake Moss

Ingredients

- 2 large eggs (120g)
- 50g plain flour
- 60g liquid honey
- 8g baking powder
- 26g caster sugar
- Green gel colour

Equipment

- Mixer or whisk
- 25cm microwave safe bowl

Place the eggs in a bowl and beat or whisk.

Add the honey to the bowl and beat until the mix is light in colour, smooth, and the whisk or beater leaves trails in the mix.

This takes about 15 minutes with a whisk so a mixer on a high setting is advised.

Beat in your food colouring.
Here I have added the light green airbrush colour. You can also use gel colours.
Add yellow for a bright and pretty moss colour or use Holly/Ivy for a deep dark colour.

This is such a fun recipe.

Careful that you don't over bake it or it will flatten down and go very rubbery.

For this batch I added dark green Progel by Rainbow Dust..
Sieve the flour and baking powder, and add all the dry ingredients to the bowl. Stir gently so you don't beat out the air. Transfer to the microwavable tupperware. Do not grease or line the container so that it sticks to the base of the bowl.

Cover the top of the container with cling film and microwave on full power for 3 1/4 minutes until the mix is well risen (Can you see around the edge is thinner, this was a one egg mix and too shallow).
Pierce and remove the cling film straight away to stop the cling film sinking onto the sponge. You want it to stick to the bottom so that it has a more natural effect when you pull it away from the container when it is cooled. Peel any smooth surfaces away for a better effect.

Completing the Design

There is something wonderful about a walk in the woodlands, listening to the wind rustling the leaves in the trees.
Adding the Honey cake moss to this cake adds another dimension to a painted cake. I add it last minute to keep it fresh.

Ingredients

- Honey cake moss in three shades of green
- White chocolate ganache coloured with green dusts
- Squires Kitchen cocoa butter
- Squires Kitchen Dust colours: eidelweiss, black, hydrangea

Equipment

- Sugarpress paint brushes
- Bowl and 20cm plate
- Palette knife

Smear the top of the cake with coconut oil and dust the surface of the cake by stippling a dry white and hydrangea mix.

Here are three colours of honey cake moss. Break them into quite large pieces and turn upside down and peel away the surface to reveal rough texture.

Place the pieces onto the cake. Begin with the darkest colour, then fit the other colours together. Fix in place with white chocolate ganache coloured with green dust and a palette knife

Here is the finished crown. I really wanted the dark patch in the centre to show the depth of the woods.

Mix black with cocoa butter and use a sugar press detail brush to paint in the pawprints. Use a larger brush and dry black dust to add more shading below the tree and below the shrubbery.

Have you ever seen an aerial photograph of a woodland?

The trees very cleverly move away from each other to avoid damage and allow light into the woodland floor.

3

Olly the Owl

"Who-Who-Who-Who is there?" said Olly the Owl. "I'm not ready to wake up yet!"

Although he looks cross now, Olly is really a kind and wise old owl. Nobody knew how long he had lived in the woods, but it must be a very long time because nobody could remember when he WASN'T there.

He had HUGE eyes, as big as the plate for your dinner!
And he saw.........and heard.......EVERYTHING!

"I'm so sorry Sir" said Cyril "But I just had to show you what I found."

"Well it is far too early to go yet. Sit and have a drink with me first" said Olly.

Cyril scampered excitedly up the tree and carefully took one of the acorn cups from Olly's branch.
"Ooh delicious!" said Cyril "Thank you so much!"

The water that tickled and trickled down through the great old tree really was very special and soooooooooooo tasty!
Cyril took a tiny sip then he couldn't wait any more, and drank it all up!

GONE!

"Yum! Thank you" said Cyril, wiping his mouth dry with his little paw.

"Hoo-Hoo-Hoo-Hoo" chuckled Olly, smiling fondly at Cyril and shaking his head.

"Come along then Cyril, you can show me what you have found".

He spread his feathery wings as wide as he could, then swooped down after Cyril.

How wide can you spread your wings?

The Armature and Assembling the Cake

Armature

- 18" x 14" MDF 18mm
- 13" x 4" MDF 12mm
- 6" round cake drums
- 5" round cake card
- M12 x 24" tall and M8 x 18" tall threaded rod both with 6 nuts & washers
- M6 18cm long threaded rod and 2 nuts & washers
- Matching spanners
- Glue gun & glue sticks
- Board covering paper
- foil & cake straws
- 2 posy pics

Equipment

- Rolling pin
- FPC sugarcraft bark mat
- PME dresden
- Cerart No.2 taper tool
- Palette knife
- Dekofee feather and veining tool
- Dusting brushes & palette
- Glue brush
- Scalpel
- Carving knife

Ingredients

- Madeira cake 5 x 6" (3 egg mix), 1 x 7" (4 egg), 1 x 8" (5 egg), 2 x 4" (2 egg) round
- 6 batches of ganache
- 3 batches of Buttercream
- 530g Renshaws chocolate brown sugarpaste

- 4kg Renshaws white decorice
- SK isomalt
- PME spray glaze
- Sugarflair airbrush colours: light green, dark green, autumn gold, brown, black
- Sugarflair nutkin brown dust
- Saracino white gel colour

- Saracino brown dust
- Squires Kitchen dusts: bulrush, chestnut, leaf green, dark green, holly ivy, daffodil, berberis
- SK bulrush liquid colour
- Edible glue
- Shredded wheat
- 120g rice krispie treats (recipe P.116)
- white icing sheet

Madeira Cake 1 egg mix (3" tall)

Ingredients

1 egg (2 oz without shell)
2 oz unsalted butter or stork margarine
2oz caster sugar
2oz self raising flour
1oz plain flour
flavouring

6" round = 3 egg mix
7" round = 4 egg mix
8" round = 5 egg mix

1. Pre-heat the oven to 150C (fan). Grease and line cake tins as in chapter 2.
2. Cream the room temperature butter or margarine in the mixer until soft and fluffy.
3. Add the sugar and beat until light.
4. Add one tablespoon of the flour then add an egg and mix until incorporated. Keep adding the rest of the eggs this way.
5. Remove from the mixer and fold in the rest of the flour gently.
6. Stir in a tablespoon of mix for a 6" round 3 egg mix and 1 tsp vanilla extract (increase or decrease accordingly for different sizes).
7. Spoon the mixture into the tin and hollow the centre a little. (For large cakes, put a metal piping nail in the base of the tin underneath the greaseproof paper (I have left the nail visible in the image above so that you can see what it looks like.
8. Bake for 1 hour to 1 hour 15 minutes
9. Leave to cool in the tin for 15 minutes then turn out upside down to cool. Rest overnight covered to cool and mature.

Assembling the Armature

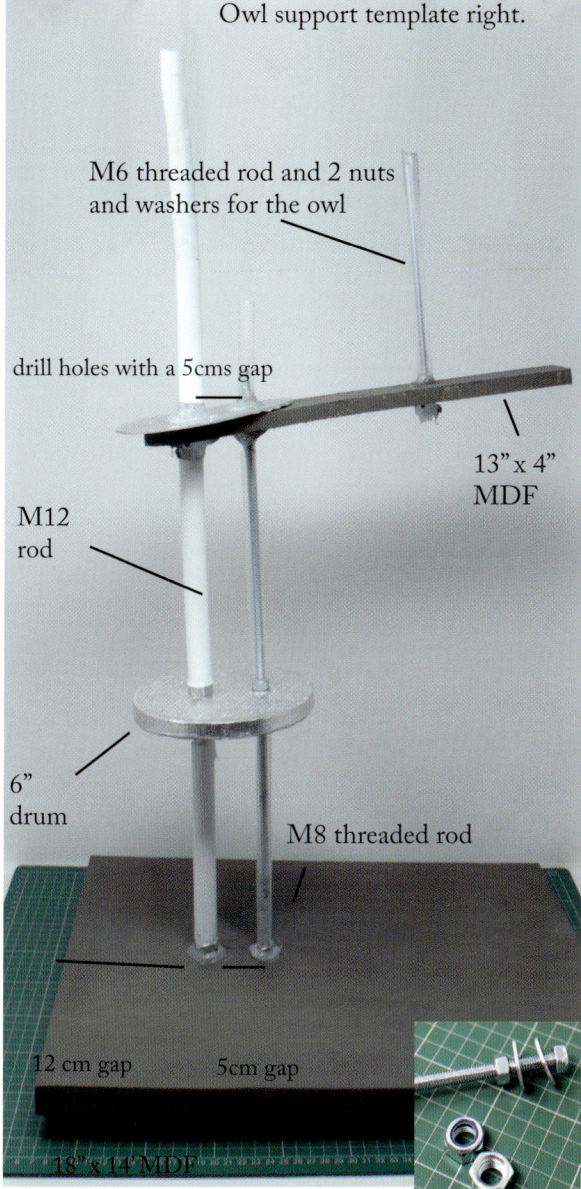

Owl support template right.

M6 threaded rod and 2 nuts and washers for the owl

drill holes with a 5cms gap

13" x 4" MDF

M12 rod

6" drum

M8 threaded rod

12 cm gap   5cm gap

18" x 14" MDF

Base
1. Glue four 2" square 18mm thick MDF feet 1" away from the bottom corners of the 18" x 14" MDF 18mm thick base board.
Drill an M12 hole 12cms away from the middle of the left hand side, and the M8 hole 5cms along from the M12 hole.
2. Onto the 13" x 4" MDF, drill the same two holes matching up with the gaps on the base board, (draw through the holes with a pencil to match it up easily) and also an M6 hole 5" away from the right hand side of the 13" x 4" MDF (9mm)

Branch Support
3. Thread an M6 nut onto the M6 threaded rod, add a washer then push down through the M6 hole of the 13" x 4" MDF. Slide a washer underneath and fix in place with a nut.
At the other end, attach the M12 rod and the M8 rod as the image, fixing a 5" cake card on top of the MDF.

Assembling the upright structure
Slide on the two cake straws next. I use the PME hollow tube dowels (white) and the others are clear cake straws. Add another nut and washer.
4. Add the 6" cake drum with the same holes drilled in half way down the remaining length then another nut and washer, then cake straws and another nut and washer.

Attaching to the base
5. To fix to the base 18" x 14" MDF 18mm thick (with the feet underneath), thread on a nut and washer onto each of the threaded rods. Push into the holes, thread another washer underneath and finish with another nut. I like to use a locking nut underneath my armatures as there is less risk of them moving.

Tighten and glue
6. Tighten all the nuts using a spanner on top and another underneath and twisting as tightly as you can.
7. Glue gun over all the nuts and washers on both sides.

Make sure you remove any glue strings from the armature before you food safe the MDF boards.

Underneath the base board

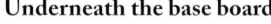

mdf foot

M8
M12
nuts

Cover the nuts and washers by painting first with piping gel then covering with board covering paper or foil. Cover the whole board and fix underneath the stand with double sided tape.

Spread buttercream at the base of the armature and begin to layer up the cake. Begin with the 8" round, then the 7" cake.

Continue stacking using the 6" cakes and buttercream as in chapter 2. Here I added more cake and carved a 6" round and the roots from the 8" square 2" deep chocolate cake to reach the top of the armature.

Use a flexible smoother to cover the main trunk with ganache. Spread a thin crumb coat from bottom to top which helps to support the cake as you work. Leave to set until touch dry, then add another layer of ganache building up to approx. 4mm thick. Neatness is not important

Making Wafer Paper Oak Leaves

Ingredients
- Saracino 0.27mm wafer paper
- Rainbow dust airbrush colour spring and holly green
- Selba fabriliquid
- Culpitt dipping solution
- Edible glue
- SK dusts: vine, leaf, dark green, holly/ivy, berberis, bulrush

Equipment
- SK oak leaf veiner
- White wires: 18, 26, 28g
- Florist tape: nile & twig
- Scissors
- Pliers
- Glue brush
- 30-50mm leaf cutters as templates or die cutter and oak leaf dies
- 2 posy pics

Airbrush the wafer paper with a mix of the spring and holly green so that the leaves are not too consistent.

Cut out the leaf shapes either using a cutter as a template and scissors or scalpel, or using paper cutting machines such as a Cricut, Cameo Silhouette or die cutters.

Paint a 1cm line of glue at the base of the leaf and add a 28g wire and place a vein on top.

I use a posy pic to put all of my flower sprays into cakes. A posy pic has a tiny hole in the bottom which is to stop choking risks, so don't block up the hole. This means that it is not safe to use a posy pic with fresh flowers as the sap could run into the cake. See P.49 for taping hints.

Hold the wired leaf against the female side of the veiner. Hold six inches away from the spout of the steamer and steam for three seconds. Line up and press the double sided veiner male side down onto the other half and hold for ten seconds until the leaf cools down. This is important, otherwise if the leaf is still too warm/damp, then it will lose all the vein as it dries. Repeat to vein all the leaves.

Tape the individual leaf stems down 1cms with quarter width nile green tape, stretching a few cms of the tape at a time and wrap around the stem tightly. Assemble the leaves in groups of two and three using half width twig colour tape. Create twists to add to the stem by twisting the tape back on itself and by binding and twisting the tape as you tape it rather than trying to make it smooth.

Create a stem by taping over a 25cm length of 18g wire with full width twig colour florist tape.
Begin by taping a large cluster on the end. Bend the stem each time you add a cluster of leaves. Twist the tape to create a tendril before attaching the leaf clusters in order to create small tendrils and extra texture on the branch. Push each branch into a posy pic and push into the trunk.

Glue gun foil to the underneath of the horizontal branch armature to achieve the rounded shape underneath. Press firmly and ensure all of the foil is fixed into place.

Shape 120g of rice krispie treats to fit the top branch shape and ganache both the foil and rice krispies.
Check the ganache is set before proceeding.

Assemble the oak leaf branches onto the tree by using posy pics and pushing the branches into the rice krispie treats on the top which will support the branches well.

Roll out 3.1kg ivory sugarpaste mixed with 530g chocolate flavoured sugarpaste. Use the mat as a template to cut your first piece (200g). Place on the mat and press firmly to indent. Heat the ganache with a blow torch or steamer and press into place.

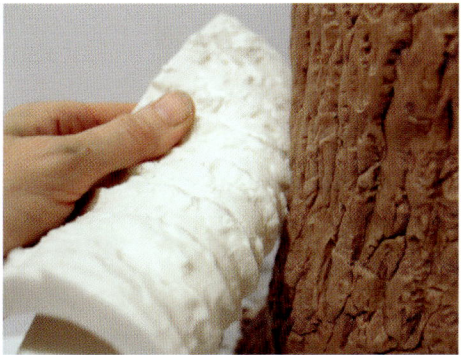

Add additional pieces, tiling them together. Blend any joins together using the bark mat rolled up into a tube. Work your way around the tree base and move up. Don't cover around the top edge or the end of the short branch yet.

Roll out 500g white sugarpaste mixed with 20g brown. Cut out circles to cover the top and the end of the branch.
Fix in place and mark the rings in using the Cerart No.2 taper tool. Add splits with the veining tool.

Complete covering the tree by covering around the cut edges. Keep the mat in place and push the cut edges against the mat for additional texture. Push the paste firmly into any indentations carved into the cake.

Roll 130g of paste into a sausage and roll in the mat. Press onto the side of the cake with the mat to add texture. Use a veining tool to add creases at the base of the branch and into the hollow.

Scrunch up kitchen foil and press onto the base of the branches to create uneven texture and age the surface of the tree.

Colouring

Airbrush black into the deep areas of the bark. Airbrush Kroma green for the moss areas then airbrush the whole tree brown. Wet a folded square of kitchen paper and sponge off colour.

Airbrush SK bulrush in the darker areas, and more green as before then sponge off the colour and leave overnight.

Dust in the recesses with bulrush and black. Airbrush shredded wheat with light green, yellow and dark green.

Pipe royal icing coloured with bulrush where you wish to place moss and push on the shredded wheat

Creating Olly the Owl

Place a 4mm tall PME tube dowel onto the threaded rod. Cut the two cake cards (template P.33) and create a hole in the centre. Push over the rod. Add an Eezee dowel which fits over the rod.

Layer the 4" cake onto the armature with the first layer a little towards the back following the template (p.32). Fix the template on with cocktail sticks and carve around the outside.

Fold down at the neck and carve the headshape as a circle when viewed from the top. Remove the template and carve in a curve down towards the tail and an hour glass shape for the owl.

Check the owl shape from each angle, ensuring there is a gentle shape to the neck. Ganache the owl. Apply the ganache first with a palette knife, then smooth with a flexi smoother as with the tree.

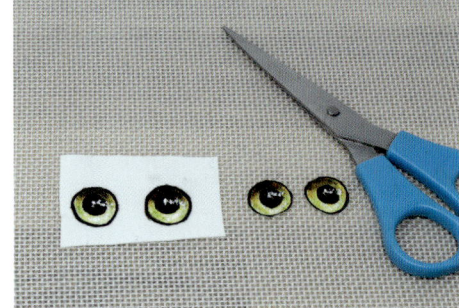

Isomalt Eyes

(Instructions to cook isomalt in chapter 8).You will need shell and shine, gloves, scissors, blow torch, silicone spatula, 19mm circle cutter, icing sheet, black food colour pen, brushes and dusts.

Paint the circle cutter with SK black mixed with dipping solution and emboss the circle. Draw over the line with the food pen. Paint the iris with sunflower, then over the top with berberis, then dots of leaf green on the sides and finally

the pupil in black, leaving small gaps in the centre. These can be painted over with white if they are not bright enough. Spray lightly with the shell and shine. Cut out the eyes with scissors or scalpel, leaving the black outline.

Put on cotton gloves and nitrile gloves on top to protect your hands. Pinch two sides of the silicone container together to create a funnel and half fill a half sphere 20mm wide mould with clear isomalt.

Place one of the hand made transfers face down into the mould on top of the clear isomalt. Press only enough so that the icing is touching the surface of the isomalt. Peel off the backing paper and pour more isomalt coloured with white

gel colouring. Allow to go cold. Remove from the mould and spray the back with glaze. Wait 1-2 minutes then blow torch the eye front briefly to return the shine. Wait another 1-2 minutes then spray the front of the eye with glaze to complete.

Hollow a 3.5cm circle around the eyes. Cover with 700g of 5mm thick sugarpaste, press into the eye hollows and pull out and fold the paste to create the two wings (or mark in the wings with a dresden).Cover the head and back with cling film to stop the paste drying out.

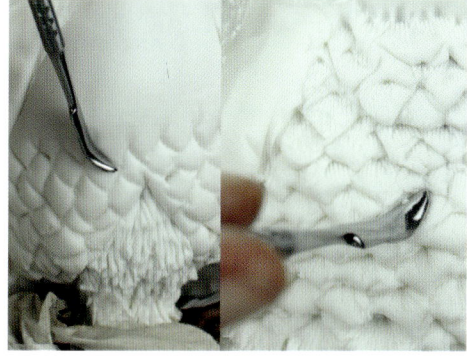

Texture the legs by dragging down the paste with the PME veining tool. Heavily indent up the centre to create two legs. Mark "v" shapes onto the body. Mark texture into the "v's" by dragging the feather tool down first on the left hand side, then down on the right.

Spray the back of the eye with glaze again and press the eyes into place in the centre of the hollows. Wrap a sausage of white paste around the socket area and indent with the PME veining tool. Mark a line to emphasise the eyebrow.

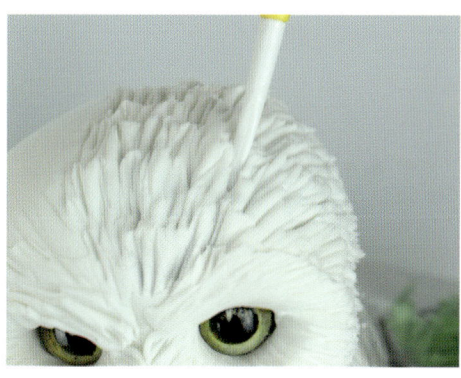

Texture the whole head with the PME veining tool, beginning from the back of the neck and working up to the top. in a fan pattern with the base point of the fan ending between the eyes.

Roll a 2.3g teardrop of flowerpaste and push in place for the beak. Texture with the Dekofee feather tool, marking from the centre ridge and down to the sides. Wrap a very thin sausage of black saracino modelling paste under the eye. Roll a slightly thicker sausage and add for the upper eye lid.

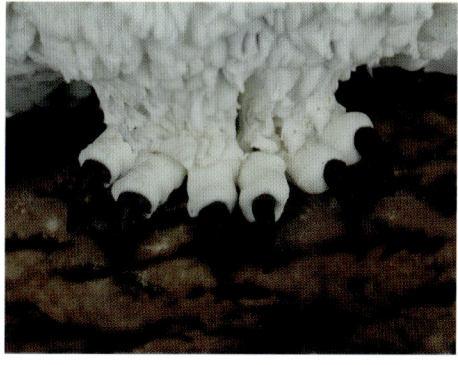

Create the claws from individual sausages of paste. Mark wrinkles with the PME veining tool. Hollow the end with the Cerart hard point. Roll thin sausages with a pointed tip from black Saracino modelling paste. Pinch a ridge down the length and fix in place for the claws.

Remove the cling film and texture the back of the owl. Mark long lines down the wings. Texture between the wings in the same way as we textured the head. Texture the wings the same way as the chest, by marking "v" shapes, then texture with feather tool.

Paint the beak with SK daffodil diluted with Culpitt dipping solution. Make it very pale. Dilute SK berberis, again pale, and paint the end of the beak. Dilute a few grains of leaf green and paint the top. Paint the beak with edible glaze.

Mix Saracino brown dust with Culpitt dipping solution. Paint the top of each of the feather marks on the chest and the wings. Paint random marks in the head and middle of back. Thicken with more dust and add depth to the top of each of the marks.

Add Sugarflair nutkin brown dust to the mix and add depth following the line of the edge of the wings front and back, also at the forehead, under the beak and at the top of the beak.

Add more nutkin brown dust and add depth following the image. Airbrush the whole owl gently with Magic Colours dark brown, emphasising between the legs, the base of the wings, under the beak and under the chin.

Spiders Web

Sprinkle 1 tbsp of vege gel and 1 tsp of CMC over 60mls water and bloom in the microwave but don't boil.
Add 2 drops of lemon juice and cool completely. Fit a No.0 nozzle to a piping bag or clay gun. Half fill with the mix. Grease acetate taped to a cake board.

Squeeze out a little mix before you touch it to the acetate to allow it to curl and straighten before you pipe the long lines of the pattern first (template on p.31). Next pipe from the centre of the web and out to the sides. If the line breaks, remove back to a line and begin to pipe again, slightly overlapping to ensure they are joined. (P.14 has piping hints)

Allow to dry for two days and fix in place initially using sterilised pins. Remove the pins one at a time and add a small amount of sugarpaste. Texture and colour the paste as you did for the rest of the tree. The gel will remain flexible if you keep it in a bag until use then it will slowly dry out to a firmer but still flexible texture.

Making Twigs

Ingredients

- Squires Kitchen pale brown flowerpaste
- Cornflour
- Squires Kitchen dusts: chestnut, bulrush, leaf green
- PME spray glaze

Equipment

- Scalpel
- Tweezers
- 2mm ball tool
- PME dresden

A twig can have so many details on it.

The two twigs were copied from an Oak tree.

So lets work on the individual details, then you can have fun creating your own twigs.

For a basic twig, colour Squires Kitchen white flowerpaste with a little bulrush dust.
Roll to a thin sausage 8cms long.
Cut one end at an angle with the scalpel and texture by pressing deep grooves in the end with the veining tool before scratching finer lines in with the scalpel.

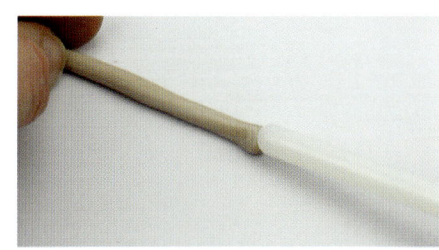

Push a bone tool in the opposite end to hollow slightly.

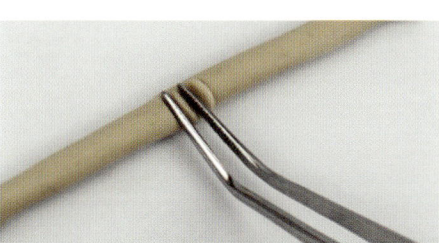

Pinch ridges in the twig with an angled tweezers.
Pinch a second ridge alongside and push them closer together with your fingers.

Mark lines and splits in the end.

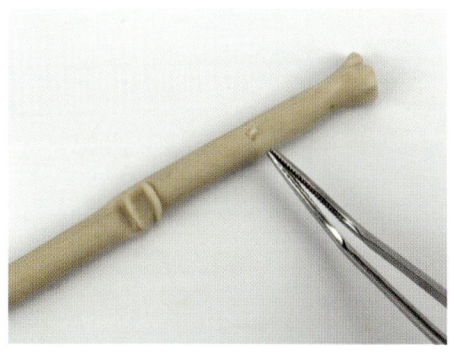

Pinch tiny nodules where the old leaves have broken off using the tweezers.
Pinch larger pieces into the sides and add texture with the veining tool.

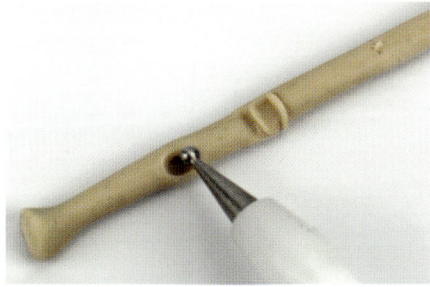

Push the Cerart ball tool into the twig to create a hollow. Pull up and to the sides to create a lip around the hollow. Texture all over with the dresden. Paint a faint wash of bulrush, then thicken the paint and add to the depth. Dust a little leaf green for moss when dry. Spray with PME spray glaze.

Seeded Grass

Ingredients

- Pale Squires Kitchen Holly/Ivy flowerpaste
- Edible glue

Equipment

- Florist tape in three shades of green
- 24, 26g white wire
- Small sharp scissors
- Florist/kitchen scissors
- Glue brush
- Dusting brush
- SK leaf green dust

Stretch out a length of florist tape.
Cut a wire to your chosen height for the grass (I used 7").

Place the wire onto the florist tape and press down firmly. Fold over the florist tape and line up before pressing firmly again. Ensure the wire is visible through the tape.

Cut the grass to a point with the scissors.

Take 2g of flowerpaste and shape into a sausage 3cms long.
Glue the end of the wire and insert right to the tip of the paste.

Start snipping from the base of the paste and up to the tip. Dust with leaf green.

Tape the blades of the grass together. Some with grass seed heads and some without.

The Woodland Floor

Spread ganache over the board using a palette knife.

Put a mixture of Bourbon and Oreo biscuits into a bag and crush with a rolling pin. Leave some lumps for texture. Scatter over the ganache.

Place dessicated coconut in the blender and blend until more broken down. Add liquid green colou and blend. Add five digestive biscuits and blend again. Add colour if too pale.

Bake three cupcakes of green coloured sponge.
Blend to crumbs.
Place on a baking tray and bake for 10 minutes.

This is 80g of the lovely filling from Bourbon Biscuits taken from a 400g packet. It is perfect for mud when kneaded. Push the grass into a rolled ball of this.

Add the twigs and scatter the brown leaves.

I believe that cupcakes are a great accompaniment to a large cake.

What better scenery than a woodland floor to display these.

4

The Adventure Begins

Olly landed silently next to the pawprint and smiled at Cyril.

"Why! It is the paw print of a cat!" said Olly, "haven't you seen one before?"

"Wow oh Wow! A cat!?.........What is that?" said Cyril, rubbing his paws together excitedly.

"Well I think you should go and ask Mr Bird who lives in the old tree stump" said Olly, "he has played with the cat before and he just MIGHT
even be able to introduce you...
.... IF you ask nicely"

What do we say to ask nicely?

"What a great idea!" said Cyril. "Thank you Sir" and off Cyril ran, his tail swishing behind him.

Cupcakes

A cupcake is perfect for any occasion.
It can be a simple individual cupcake or made to look very special .

Ingredients

- 110g softened butter or stork
- 110g caster sugar
- 110g McDougalls sponge flour
- 2 large eggs
- ½ tsp vanilla extract

Equipment

- Muffin tray
- Large mixing bowl
- Wooden spoon or mixer
- Ice cream scoop
- Cake tester or skewer

The most important thing when baking is bringing your ingredients to room temperature otherwise your batter might split.

Method

1. Heat oven to 160c fan/gas 4
2. Beat the ingredients together in a bowl.
3. Use an ice cream scoop to portion the cakes into the cupcake cases.
4. Bake for 15 minutes until golden brown and a skewer comes out clean.
5. Cool on a cooling rack

Use an ice cream scoop to fill the cupcake cases to half way

Alternative flavourings

- Coffee - Dilute 1 tsp coffee in 1 tablespoon of milk
- lemon or orange - add fresh grated zest
- 1/2 tsp almond essence
- Tablespoons of sprinkles
- Simple Chocolate - Replace 1 tbsp flour with 1 tbsp of Cocoa Powder
- Chocolate chip - 1 tbsp of chocolate chips
- Marble - Make double the quantity of vanilla and chocolate and put half a scoop of each into the cupcake case then swirl with the cake tester.

**Peeling cases?
This can be caused by under-filling the cases or by under-baking.
Metallic cases are the easiest to use**

Pawprint Cupcakes

Ingredients

- Cupcakes
- Renshaw chocolate brown flavoured
- Sugarpaste
- Vanilla Buttercream
- Strawberry jam
- Icing sugar shaker

Equipment

- Sugar Press cat pawprint
- Small rolling pin
- Apple/cupcake corer or wooden spoon
- Two tea spoons
- Piping bag
- Small sharp knife
- 7.5cm circle cutter
- Nail brush

This is a fantastic project that suits the beginner, baking with a small child, or a super quick cupcake for those with a business.

You can personalise it using colour for the topper and with your flavour for the cupcake and the frosting .

Why not add an extra surprise of jam or ganache in the core of the cupcake before you put the top of the cupcake on.

But bear in mind that runny jams or liquids will disappear into the cupcake.

Core the cupcake either with the apple/cupcake corer, or by gently twisting the back of a wooden spoon inside.
Use two teaspoons to fill with thick jam.

Roll out sugarpaste on icing sugar. Texture with a nail brush and emboss the pawprint. Cut out the shape with the circle cutter.

Pipe buttercream onto the top of the cupcake. Chill until the buttercream is firm to touch then place the pawprint on top.

Blackberries

Ingredients

- Squires Kitchen flower paste: white, holly/ivy
- Squires Kitchen dust colour: sunflower, vine green, leaf green, bulrush, violet, holly/ivy; black
- Squires Kitchen edible glue
- Cornflour
- PME Spray glaze
- PME petal base or trex

Equipment

- Lacemakers cotton
- White florist wires: 24g, 26,28g
- Nile green florist tape
- Culpitt micro matt head stamen
- FMM small calyx cutter
- Tinkertech 96 blossom cutter
- Glue brush
- No.8 filbert dusting brush
- Celpad
- FMM rose leaf Cutters 2,5, 3, 4cm
- Squires Kitchen GJ Bramble Veiners3.5,4,6.5cm
- CK grooved board
- Squires Kitchen veining tool
- Large metal ball tool

This is a lovely cupcake to put together. Texture the earth as for the pawprint cupcake, but add a mixture of crushed green biscuits and coconut before adding the blackberry in a posy pic.

The Flower

Stamen Centre

Wrap lacemakers cotton 30 times around two fingers, then twist into a figure of eight.
Take a one third length of 28g white florist wire and insert through one side of the loop. Twist to attach, then add another wire at the opposite side of the loop.
Tape 3 cms of the stems with quarter width of nile green florist tape, ensuring that you cover the wire loop around the cottons.Cut the loop in half and neaten the top of each to a curve.

Outer Ring of Stamen
Dust the inner stamen with a mix of SK sunflower and a touch of vine green.

Tape twelve micro matt head stamen randomly around the centre. You can also glue.
Glue the tips and dip in SK bulrush dust.

Flower
Grease your board with PME petal base. Thinly roll out white flowerpaste and cut out the blossom cutter. Remove a wedge from between the petals with a scalpel.

Dust the board with cornflour and vein and texture the petals by rolling from the middle to the left, and the middle and to the right with the Squires Kitchen veining tool.

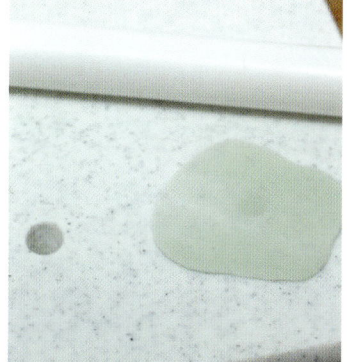

Flower Calyx
Rub petal base on the middle size of the tiny bumps in the Celboard and press on a piece of pale green holly/ivy. Roll thinly with a celpin.

Remove the paste from the board, line up the FMM small calyx cutter over the hip and cut. Swipe your thumb over the paste while still in the cutter to remove jagged edges.

Dusting
First dust with leaf green, then mix the leaf green with a little holly/ivy and dust the centre. Dust the edges gently with violet.

Turn the flower shape face down, glue the centre and fix the calyx in place with the sepals and tepals of the calyx supporting the petals.

Glue the centre of the calyx, and gently thread the prepared stamen centre through, twisting clockwise as you pull it through. This will anchor the wire into the paste, whereas twisting side to side would create a gap in the paste around the wire. Settle the stamen into the centre of the flower.

Buds
Roll a small pea of white paste into a teardrop and insert a hooked one quarter length of 28g white wire. Tape the stem with quarter width nile green tape. Roll out the remaining pale green SK sfp very thinly. Cut out an FMM small calyx cutter taking care that the edges are clean. Place on a flower pad and thin the edges with a ball tool. Place the shape face down on kitchen roll. Dust with moss green and a little aubergine on the edges. Fix in place behind the bud.
Tape the buds together in groups taped 1cm below the bud.

The Leaf

Lightly grease the board with petal base or Trex or Crisco and remove the excess with kitchen paper. Roll out SK light green holly/ivy paste into a sausage and firmly flatten onto the groove.

Roll the paste from bottom to top until it is thin enough to see the dots on the board. Remove the paste and turn the paste over to reveal the veined side of the paste and place onto the smooth side of the board ready to cut.

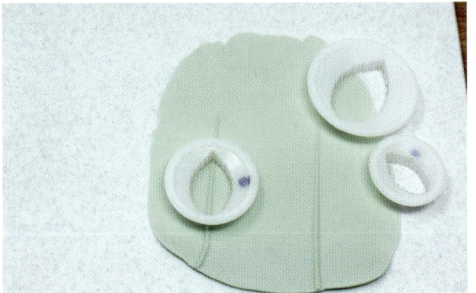

Use the rose leaf cutters, line up with the vein and press firmly onto the paste and wiggle the cutter slightly. Remove the cutter with the paste still in it and rub your thumb over the edges to remove the excess paste and avoid rough edges to the leaf.

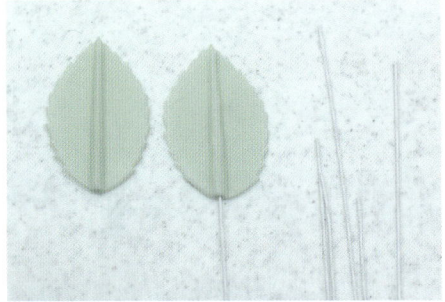

Moisten the wire with edible glue, wiping the excess on the back of your hand, and holding the leaf between finger and thumb, insert the 28g wire 2/3rds up the leaf. If you want an even better finish, only push the wire up into the leaf 3-4mm but this will need supporting while it dries. I vein a piece of foil and rest it in there to dry.

Place the leaf right side up on a flower pad and using a large ball tool, thin the edges by stroking the ball tool up the side of the leaf half on and half off. If you see a ridge on the edge, you missed the edge.

Cut your wires on an angle to make it easier to insert into the paste.

Veining the Leaf

Lightly dust the veiner with cornflour (shake off excess) place the indented half of the veiner onto the work surface and line up your leaf so that the groove from the board sits inside the hollowed vein of the veiner. Take the protruding vein half of the veiner and carefully line up onto the other half of the veiner and press firmly. Remove carefully by peeling back the veiner rather than pulling the wire. Shape the leaf by pinching back the tip. Leave until leather dry to make dusting easier.

Colouring the Leaf

Dust the leaf first with leaf green using the flat side of a number 8 filbert brush. Dust from the base of the leaf to the tip with the flat side of the brush, avoiding stabbing the colour onto the leaf. Brush from base to tip and always return the brush to the base each time to avoid a striped finish.

Overdust with holly/ivy, leaving the top edges with less colour. Overdust the front top edges and one side of the back of the leaf with violet. Brush across the veins to catch the details with the colour.

Spray lightly with PME Spray glaze in short bursts rather than lsng continuous spraying. Aim for a natural leaf shine rather than a glossy finish.

Assembling the Leaves

Tape 5mm of each of the smaller leaves with quarter width nile green tape. Begin to tape by placing a small amount of the stretched tape onto your finger, place the wired leaf firmly onto the tape and with your finger and thumb of the other hand firmly twist. Keep the tape at a 25 degree angle to keep the tape from building up too quidly. Attach tape to the large leaf and tape down until you have a small leaf width gap, then add the small leaves in pairs, each leaning outwards. Tape groups of leaves opposite each other.

Dust the stems with a little more leaf green and violet. Spray the assembled leaves lightly with the PME spray glaze.

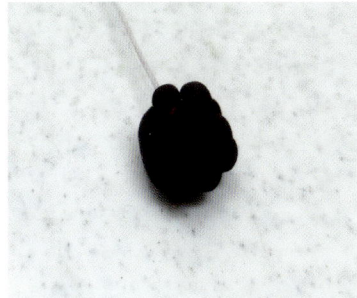

Berries

Bend a shepherds hook on the end of a one third length of white 24g wire. Roll 3g of black SK sfp into a cone shape. Heat the hook of the wire in a candle for ten seconds, then carefully insert the hook into the rounded base of the cone until the hook is buried halfway up the cone. Count to twenty to allow the wire to cool down and neaten the shape of the base. Set aside to dry preferably overnight, but it can work for smaller buds after ten minutes.

Roll a minimum of 30 very small balls of black SK sfp. Mix black flowerpaste with edible glue to make a very sticky chewing gum like consistency and paint this gunge over the cone. Fix the black balls all over.

To create the shine, you can either dip the berries in full strength glaze and shake off the excess or spray with Shell and Shine. Leave to dry.

Make a calyx for the berry as for the flower. Glue the centre of the calyx, and slide the wire of the blackberry into place, pulling the sepals and tepals of the calyx backwards.

No time?

Why not use the SK blackberry mould instead.

Dust the mould with cornflour, Fill one side, press in the 24g wire, then fill the other side and glue together. I cut it in half to do this method.

Final Assembly

Tape berries into clusters of 2,3,4, joining them approximately 1cm below the berry. The flowers can also be joined together in the same way, but take care not to damage the petals. Tape the prepared clusters of flowers, berries and buds together approximately 3cms down the stem as in the image right. Tape the leaves with either two or three sets of leaves at the same point around the stem to allow them to sit neatly in the cupcake. Always remember to use a food safe posy pic.

Sammy The Snail

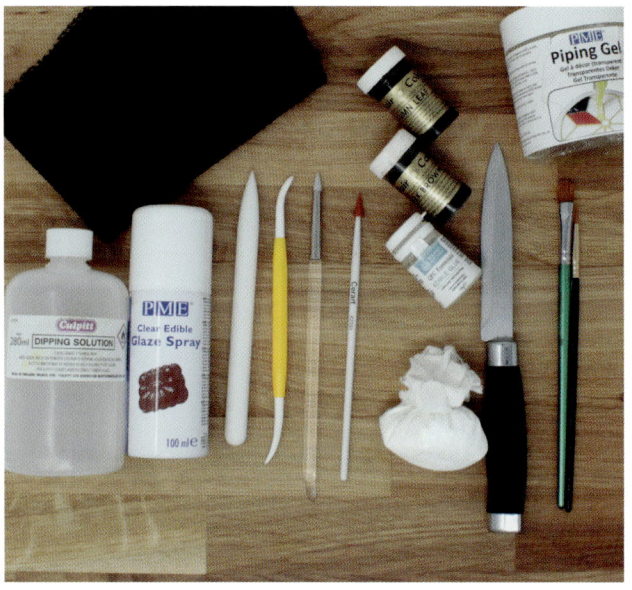

Ingredients

- 1g Squires Kitchen white flowerpaste
- 35g white Saracino pasta model
- Sugarflair paste colour: dark brown, autumn leaf
- Culpitt dipping solution
- PME spray glaze
- PME piping gel
- SK edible lue
- Cornflour puff

Equipment

- PME dresden
- Celpin
- Cerart No.2 soft taper
- Cerart K2220 hard point
- Sharp knife
- No.8 Filbert brush
- Glue brush
- Non slip matting

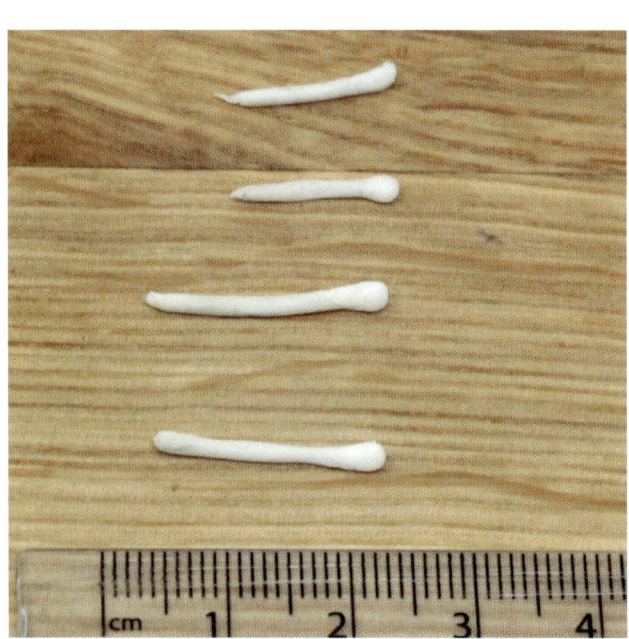

Roll 2 x 2cms with a slight bulb on one end for the major eye tentacles and 2 x 1cm tentacles for the lower minor tentacles from the Squires Kitchen flower paste.

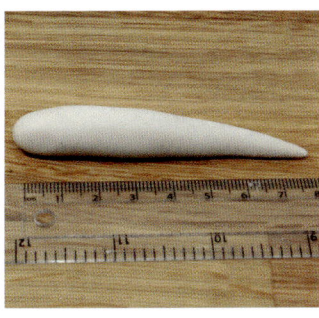

Colour the Saracino light brown with Sugarflair dark brown. Roll 10.5g to an 8cms long teardrop for the body.

Texture the shape with non slip matting.

Pinch under the head between your finger and thumb to create the ridge as in the image above.

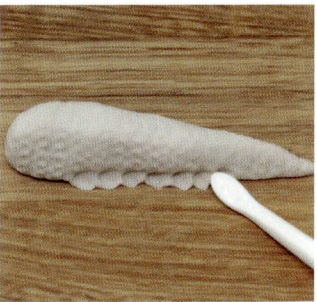

To create the sole or foot, press the PME dresden in to the base of the paste and stroke away from the body.

Create the eye holes by pushing in the Cerart K2220 tool.

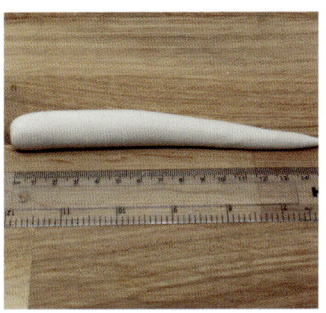

Roll the shell from 24g of the same colour paste and to 15cms long.
Ensure the shape is tapered.

Coil the shell starting at the narrow pointed end. Curl back the wide end of the shell to create the mantle. Sit on the celpin to hollow underneath.

Use the No.2 soft taper tool to gently mark lines across the shell and emphasising the apex of the shell (the centre of the whorl).

Gently push the tentacles into place. The major tentacles (the eyes), will be the top ones.

Paint stripes of autum leaf and dark brown straight from the pot onto the shell.

Dilute a mix of the two colours with Culpitt dipping solution and wash the colour onto the body and tentacles.

Use the same wash and add a little more dark brown to paint the shell. Painting across it rather than from head to toe.
Spray with PME spray glaze.

5

The Meeting

"Where is Mr Bird?" said Cyril to himself.
"WHERE IS HE!"

Too many trees had been cut down and that meant that there were now too
many tree stumps, so it was very hard to find the right tree stump.
"Stupid humans!" Cyril said angrily.

Suddenly, Cyril stopped very still and listened.....................
"What is that beautiful song I can hear? That must be him!"

"Well hello young Cyril, you are getting very grown-up now" said Mr Bird.

"Excuse me sir! But I am eight moons now!
Only one more moon and I will be fully grown!"
Cyril folded his arms crossly over his chest.

"Oh I do beg your pardon young man! My eyes aren't as good as they used to be.
Now, how can I help?" Mr Bird smiled at Cyril.

"Olly the Owl said you might be able to introduce me to the cat
that has visited our woods"
Cyril stretched up so big and tall waiting eagerly for Mr Bird to answer.

"I know just the person who can help you" said Mr Bird "you need the old man from the
cottage at the edge of the woods.   The cat lives there with him".

"Thank you very much Mr Bird" said Cyril
"Soon, I will meet the cat!"

Cyril and Mr Bird

Ingredients

- 2 x 6"R morello cherry madeira (recipe p.32)
- 400g buttercream (add 1tsp almond extract and replace 50g of icing sugar with 50g ground almonds)
- Morello cherry jam
- 900g dark chocolate ganache
- 800g white Renshaws decor ice
- 50g Renshaw choc brown sugarpaste
- CMC
- Dust colours: SK sunflower, berberis, chestnut, bulrush
- Dust colours: Saracino: yellow, red, green, brown, black, white, skintone.
- Dust colours: Sugarflair: nutkin brown
- PME spray glaze
- Saracino liquid shiny
- 25g rice krispie treats (recipe P.116)
- 140g SK white flowerpaste (bird and toadstool)

Equipment

- Rolling pin
- Small sharp knife
- Palette knife
- White wires: 18, 20, 24, 26g
- Kebab skewer
- Florist tape: white, brown, nile green
- Scalpel
- Bone tool

- PME dresden
- Cerart K2220 hard point
- Flexi smoothers
- Sharp tweezers
- Detail brush
- Palette
- Dusting brushes
- Aluminium foil

- Sugar City fern cutter and veiner set
- Pliers
- Celpad
- Cling film
- 2" circle cake card
- FPC Sugarcraft bark mat
- FPC Sugarcraft 3D bird mould

Squirrel Armature

Push two kebab skewers (or 16g wires) into spare polystyrene.
Place the template against the skewers to check the position.
Twist 2 x 24g white wires tightly around the kebab skewers and twist to the end.

Twist another 24g wire around the top of the kebab skewers to straighten the top of the kebab skewers and fix them together.

Tape over the wires with white florist tape.

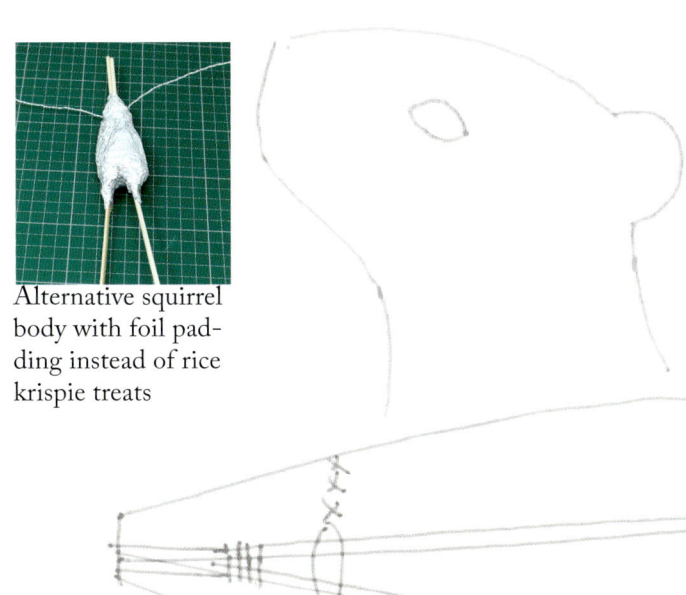

Alternative squirrel body with foil padding instead of rice krispie treats

Squirrel head actual size template formed from sugarpaste.
If putting a cone inside, ensure the shape including sugarpaste is still this size.

Actual size template for internal rice krispie or foil armature body. Please note. The Paste added to this shape will increase the finished width by 1.5cm.
Feet are 1.5cm tall and are added later.

Squeeze 25g of rice krispie treats tightly on the armature until it matches the template. Wrap in cling film and leave until set.

The Tree Trunk Cake

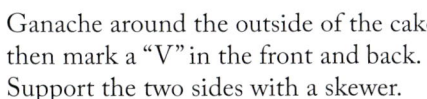

Bake 2 x 6" round Madeira cakes (recipe p.32, add 1tsp cherry extract per 6" cake and marble with Rainbow Dust claret progel).Fill with almond buttercream (Add 1 tsp almond extract to a full buttercream batch and replace 50g icing

sugar with ground almonds) and morello cherry jam.

Ganache around the outside of the cake then mark a "V" in the front and back. Support the two sides with a skewer.

Carve down to remove the cake. Make the front V to be a larger gap that the back. Ganache the inside and allow to set.

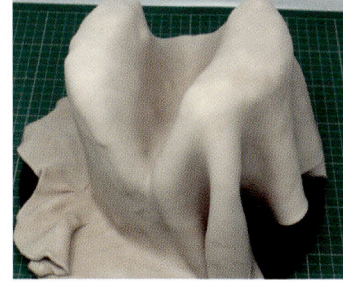

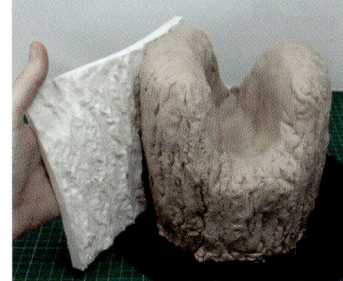

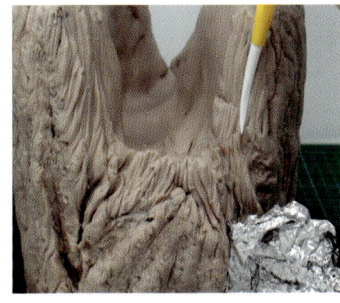

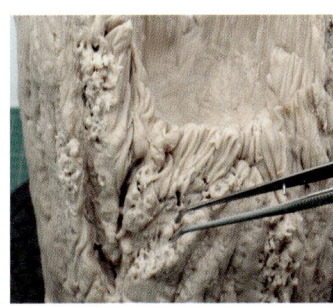

Mix 650g white & 50g brown sugarpaste, cover the cake all in one. Smooth carefully into the hollow using a pad of paste.

Texture the sides using the FPC bark mat. Gently press against one side of the cake, while supporting the other.

Draw the PME dresden veining tool from the base up to create deeper lines. Press scrunched foil into the indentations for texture.

Pinch and pull the moss texture into the paste using pointed tweezers.

Deepen the lines on the front of the trunk using the veining tool and a scalpel.

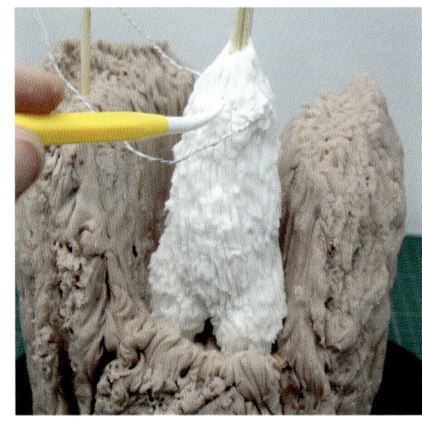

Covering the Body

Push the squirrel armature into place in the cake. Wrap in cling film and leave to set either in the fridge for an hour or overnight. Roll out 150g of white sugarpaste and wrap around the body of the squirrel to cover., squeezing into place to fix. Scratch and drag the fur texture down the body with a scalpel, using the PME veining tool to create deeper texture.

The Head

Form the squirrel head shape from 55g white sugarpaste with a pinch of CMC added. Pinch the muzzle area of the squirrel slightly narrower than the head itself. Push the front of the muzzle gently with a finger to flatten and gently push the chin area a little more. Treat the nose of the squirrel as the centre of a clock and use a scalpel to scratch the fur texture onto the squirrel always moving away from the nose from front to back for fine fur, or start at the back and moe towards the front for more texture..

Push a small PME ball tool in for the eyes.
Pull to a slight almond shape using the PME veining tool.
Push the PME small ball tool back into the eye socket and gently hollow out the eyelid a little by pulling and hooking it forward.

Indent the line for the mouth with a scalpel, pulling the lower lip down a little before shaping the lip.
Add a tiny piece of white paste for the nose, marking in the nostrils with the Cerart K2220 hard point tool.

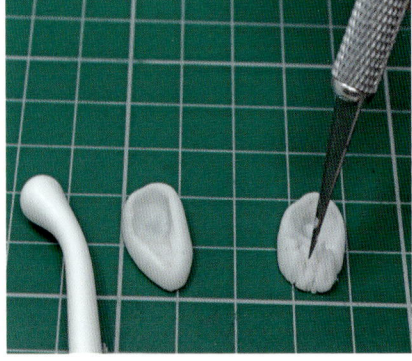

Roll 2 x 1g balls of sugarpaste with CMC added into teardrops.
Hollow with a bone tool.
Pinch up the fur at the base of the ear and slice the paste with a scalpel to create fur at the base of the ear.

Push into the head with the Cerart K2220 hard point tool to create a hollow for the ears.
Glue inside the hollow and wait for 30 seconds before pushing in the ears.
Insert the K2220 tool inside the ears to ensure they are fixed, then texture where the ears join the head with a scalpel to blend the join.

The Arms

Roll 15g of sugarpaste to a skittle shape 7cms long with the wider end at the shoulder. Slide onto the wire and firmly blend onto the body. Scratch down the arm to texture and divide the paw into four fingers.

Dust the Tree Trunk

Start by dusting the Saracino yellow dust onto the tree trunk with a half inch wide brush.

To add the depth, dust Sugarflair nutkin brown dust into the hollows.

Mix Saracino yellow and green together and overdust the yellow moss patches.

Dust the rest of the log with Saracino brown. Don't worry about making the colour even as it will look more natural. Take care not to dust over the moss, but it will pick up some of the colour naturally.

Overdust the log with Sugarflair nutkin brown and Saracino black. Emphasise the moss areas with the yellow/green mix,
(the browns that accidentally overdust the moss will have added to the effect).
Dust small areas of the moss with Saracino green before adding a little white where you wish the log to look bleached.
Spray the whole log with PME spray glaze to set the colour.

Dusting the Squirrel

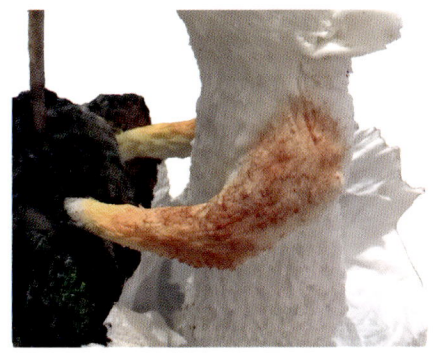

Dust the fore arms of the squirrel from wrist up to elbow with SK sunflower and a half inch wide brush. Gently stroking the dust along the arm rather than scrubbing it in or you may damage the fur texture.

Overdust the whole arm with SK berberis mixed with SK chestnut. Ensure that the lower arm shows a little of the SK sunflower colour and gradually blends. Dust up to the shoulder.

Overdust the upper arm with SK chestnut to darken.

Dust the body with SK chestnut and up to the top of the head.

Take care to avoid dusting the ear, chin, and eye area.

Dust the inner ears with Saracino skintone, then mix skintone with SK berberis and SK sunflower to dust the outer ear. Dust inside the mouth with SK chestnut.

Dust inside the ears with SK chestnut.

Overdust the body with SK bulrush including emphasising the line around the belly edge.

Wet a folded piece of kitchen paper and lightly sponge the body to remove a small amount of colour and allow to dry.

NB The kitchen roll in the image was put there to protect the inside of the tree trunk from the dust colours on the squirel.

Roll a 35g ausage of pale beige SK flowerpaste and fix onto the wire for the mushroom stem. Place the cake card on top, sliding to sit on the stem. Push a small ball of black paste in for the squirrels eye and add lower then upper eyelids from white paste.
Dust the nose with a little Saracino skintone and lightly overdust with SK chestnut

Flatten a 35g ball of SK pale beige flowerpaste and press into place for the mushroom cap.
Cover the underside of the cap with more beige paste, glueing into place and texture the lines into place with a PME veining tool.

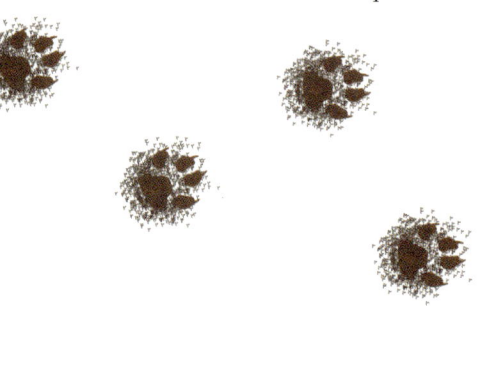

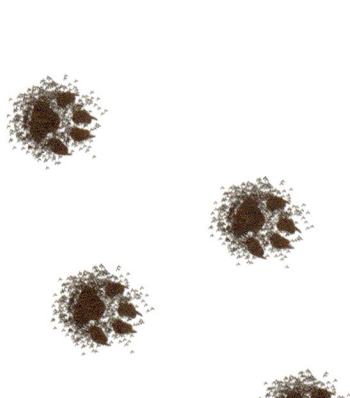

Mr Bird

Tape over two lengths of 24g wire with brown florist tape.
Cut and bend the birds toes to the template in the life sized picture below including the thicker 18g wire also taped with brown florist tape.

Lay your wires over these to check for size.

Tape the legs and support wire into place as shown in the picture above.

Finished leg left is life sized

The FPC bird mould

Repeat to make a second leg and tape the two legs together at the top.

Tape the one leg in place using the protruding wire above the mushroom cap.

Fill the two parts of the FPC bird mould with 23.5g of Squires Kitchen flower paste each, paint glue on one side and press together while they are both still in the mould.
De-mould by gently pushing out of the top mould.
Pull the head gently forward and down a little.

Wrap small sausages of paste around the top of the leg and texture with a scalpel. Add a black ball for each eye and a slightly longer beak. Scratch extra texture into the chest of the bird with a scalpel. Mould the wings using 3.3g of flower paste each and fix into place.
Dust the squirrel body again with SK berberis. Dust the mushroom stalk, top and edge of cap with SK chestnut.

Push a skewer or two wires into the squirrels base.
Concertina a square of foil, like folding a fan, and wrap around the tail to thicken.

Wrap sugarpaste around the foil and squeeze to fix.
Blend the paste onto the body with a PME dresden.
Texture with the PME veining tool from base of tail to tip.
Snip the whole tail with scissors.
Lightly dust the tail with SK berberis and SK chestnut.

Lightly dust the birds tail and end of wings with Saracino black.
Mix the black with Culpitt dipping solution and paint the darker patches on the bird, allowing them to fade away at the edges, following the feature direction.
Lightly dust under the belly of the bird with SK chestnut and around the squirrels eye. Paint white dots on the eyes of the squirrel and bird.

Ladybird

Lightly flatten the base of a 1g oval of red flowerpaste.
Indent a line to mark the head and another along the length of the body.
Dust the body of the ladybird with Saracino red.
Mix Saracino black with Saracino liquid shiny and paint the head and the line down the back.
Paint the eyes with white
Fix into place with glue.

The Paws

Roll a 2g ball of sugarpaste with CMC into an oval.
Cut four fingers by removing three triangle wedges and attach for the front paws. (Create two more in the same way but with five toes for the back paws.)
Texture slightly with a scalpel, and dust the top of the paws first with sunflower, then berberis and chestnut. Dust the nails with black.
Steam the finished piece or use PME spray glaze to set all the colours on the trunk, bird and squirrel.

Fern

Ingredients

- SK Holly/Ivy flowerpaste
- SK dust colours: berberis, fern, leaf green, aubergine

Equipment

- Sugar City Fern Leaf veiner 6cm
- Sugar city fer leaf cutters e, 3.5 and 5cm
- Cel pad
- Ball tool
- Wire cutters
- Wires: 20,28g white
- Nile green florist tape

Pin out pale green flowerpaste (colour with SK fern dust) with a gentle ridge down the centre (as in chapter three). Cut the Sugar City fern cutter shapes and wire with quarter length pieces of 28g white wires. Thin the edges on a celpad with a ball tool.

Vein in the Sugar City double sides veiner and pinch into shape.

Dust the shapes first with SK fern, then over dust at the base with SK leaf green. Dust the backs with SK berberis.

The gap for each leaf can be determined by the width of the leaf you are about to add.

Take a full length 20g white wire and begin to tape the individual fern leaves in place. Tape one second to smallest leaf on the end with no wire showing, then add from smallest to largest in pairs.

Bend the stem into a gentle and natural curve.

Dust the stem with SK leaf green and SK aubergine.

Push into place on the cake using a posy pic to protect the cake from the wires.

6

Mr Morris

Mr Morris was the friendly old man who lived in the pretty tumble-down cottage on the edge of the woods. His garden was a little bit too wild than it should be now, but he was kind to all the animals and birds in the Green Oak Woods and he always kept tasty treats for them.

As Cyril got closer to the tall brown fence, he started to move a little slower.

"I have never been this far away from my tree before" he thought to himself.
He was a little bit scared now as well as excited, but...... "A cat! I have to meet the cat!"

Bravely he puffed out his chest and crept closer to the fence.

Suddenly, the old man appeared. He leaned his arm on the top of the fence, and peered down at Cyril.
"We haven't met before" said the old man "I'm Mr Morris. Have you come a long way?"

"Please sir!" said Cyril "I have come all the way from the big tree by the clearing, SUCH a long way!"

"You must be a very brave young squirrel" said Mr Morris smiling, "welcome to my garden"

Cyril WAS very proud of himself.
He had asked for help..... and followed the directions..... AND made it all the way to the old mans cottage! Not bad for a squirrel of only eight moons.

"So why have you come all this way?" asked Mr Morris.

"Why, I heard that the cat lives here, and I have never met a cat before." By now, Cyril was VERY excited.

"I can definitely help you! The cat is called Luna, and she lives with me in my little cottage.   Would you like to meet her?" asked Mr Morris.

"Oh yes please Sir!" cried Cyril, "That would be wonderful!"

Sugar Ivy

Ingredients

- Squires Kitchen holly/ivy flowerpaste
- Edible Glue
- Cornflour

- Sugarflair dusts: moss green, foliage green, forest green, aubergine
- PME Spray Glaze

- Orchard ivy cutters 2, 2.5, 3, 3.75cm
- White florist wires: 24, 26, 28g
- Florist tape: nile green, beige, brown
- Scissors
- Wire cutters
- Large metal ball tool
- Glue brush

- No.8 filbert dusting brush
- Flower pad
- Grooved board
- Squires Kitchen gracillas ivy veiners 4.5cm
- PME scalpel
- PME Scribe

Unwired Leaves

Rub a non-stick board with trex and use a piece of kitchen towel to remove the excess. Roll out pale green Squires Kitchen flowerpaste thinly.
Lift up off the board and place back down. Cut out a selection of ivy leaf shapes.

Place the leaf on a flower pad and using a ball tool, thin the edges with the ball half on and half off the leaf shape.
If you find a ridge on the edge of the leaf, it means you did not have the ball tool over the edge but slightly inside it.
Lightly dust the Squires Kitchen gracillas ivy leaf veiner with corn flour.

Place the leaf in the veiner and press firmly. Gently shape the leaf and leave to dry on squashed kitchen paper for four hours until they are leather dry.

Wired Leaves

Groove board method on P44 or the ridge method on P76. Cut 26g white wires at an angle and in quarters for the large leaves and 28g white wires for the smaller leaves. Glue the leaf, wipe off the excess and insert into the lower third of the leaf pinching the leaf between finger and thumb. Thin the edges with a ball tool on a cel pad. Pinch into shape.

I think there is nothing nicer than edible foliage on a cake that looks as if it just grew there.

The more natural the better.

Allow to dry until they are leather dry and begin to dust.
This is the same for wired and for the unwired leaves.
First with Sugarflair moss green, then overdust with Sugarflair foliage green, forest green, then Sugarflair aubergine before spraying two coats with the PME spray glaze.

When touch dry, use a scribe to scratch the veins in by drawing the scribe along the veins created by the veiner. For the wired leaves, Tape 5cms of each wired ivy stem with quarter width nile tape.

Bud leaves
Take a 3cm length of half width nile green tape and pinch the tip to a point, twist the tape one centimetre below the point to be the leaf, then tape onto a 28g wire.

Tendrils
Tape 6cms down a 24g wire with beige tape and bend and twist it for a tendril. Twist the end of the tape to a 1cm long tendril and tape in the little bud you created.

Tape down this stem to the point that you would like to add in leaves as in the large image.
Make a number of these to add in to your main stem.

Beginning with a twisted beige taped 24g white wire, add a small leaf with 1cm of its stem showing then tape down 6cms. I added in another section with the bud leaf on a twist shown above and a medium leaf. The leaves can be added in pairs or individually. A fresh example of ivy is always the best thing to follow.

Wafer Paper Wild Dog Rose

Ingredients
- Saracino 0.27mm white wafer paper
- SK dusts: sunflower, berberis, chestnut, bulrush, vine, leaf, holly/ivy green
- Culpitt dipping solution
- Selba fabriliquid
- SK white flowerpaste
- Rainbow Dust airbrush colour spring green, holly/ivy rose

Equipment
- Airbrush
- Scissors
- Aldaval dog rose petal & leaf veiners
- Filbert dusting brushes
- Culpitt micro matt stamen
- Nile green florist tape
- SK daisy centre mould
- Wires 28, 30g

Airbrush the wafer paper with Rainbow Dust rose pink colour. Cut the petal templates using the template. Cut a 1cm slit in the bottom of the petal. Glue one side of the join and fix a one third length of 30g white wire. Glue the join and overlap to cover the wire.

Spray the petal from 6" away with one squirt of Fabriliquid. Wait approximately 30 seconds for the fabriliquid to absorb then vein the rose in the Aldaval wild rose veiner (as in chapter 3).

Bend a hook in a 28g white wire. Place a tiny ball of pale yellow flowerpaste in the veiner. Glue the hook and push into the paste. Squeeze into place.

**The templates for the rose petal, calyx and bract are on the ingredients list.
The leaf templates are on the bottom line of text.**

Cut micro stamen into small bunches or 6-7 small seed head stamen. Tape the centre with sunflower and a tiny dust of vine green. Touch the centre with berberis. Mix berberis with Culpitt dipping solution and paint the end of the stamen. Mix the bulrush with dipping solution and paint 2-3 of the stamen tips.

Wire and vein the leaves as the petals. Dust with moss green and catch the tips with aubergine. Tape the large leaf at the tip and the other size leaves in pairs going down the stem.

Tape the petals around the centre, tucking the second petal underneath the first, repeating until all are in place. Tape down the stem. Assemble by taping the leaves one above the rose and one either side at the base. Dust the stem with moss and aubergine.

Fault Line Cake

Coffee & Walnut Sponge

Ingredients

- 300g Stork margarine
- 300g caster sugar
- 300g 6 large eggs
- 300g McDougalls sponge flour sifted
- 2 tsp coffee
- 3 tbsp milk
- 55g crushed walnuts

Equipment

- 12" square Silverwood multi-size tin
- Greaseproof paper
- Mixer

Method

1. Weigh out all the room temperature ingredients and place into your mixing bowl (reserve the walnuts and coffee milk for now).

2. Mix the ingredients together, taking care not to overbeat.

3. Stir in the coffee milk and the walnuts

4. Line the Silverwood multisize cake tins to bake four 6" cakes at the same time. The metal dividers will conduct the heat and help the cakes to cook. Line each section individually.

5. Bake at 170C / gas 5 in four 6" square tins for 25-30 minutes. Cool on a rack.

6. When baked, remove the side and middle side strips to allow the cake to cool on a baking tray.

I always line my cake tins by greasing the tin and lining with greaseproof.
It is particularly important when a multisize tin or a loose ring so that the mix does not leak. Follow the instructions in chapter two and treat each of the four sections as an individual tin.

Coffee and Walnut Buttercream

Beat 250g room temperature unsalted butter for 2-3 minutes until light and fluffy, then beat in 550g sieved icing sugar and 1tbsp coffee mixed with 2tbsp milk.
Mix for 30 seconds to 1 minute.

In hot weather, replace 100g of the icing sugar with royal icing sugar.

Split and Fill the Fault Line Cake

Ingredients

- Saracino 0.27mm wafer paper
- 1.25kg Renshaws chocolate brown sugarpaste
- Saraino dusts: yellow, green, brown, black
- Ganache
- Cocoa powder
- Oreo & Bourbon

Equipment

- Nail brush
- Ruler
- Small rolling pin
- Wide paintbrushes
- Smoother
- Sharp knife
- PME scalpel
- PME scribe
- PME dresden
- Scissors
- Spirit level
- Cocktail sticks

Spread buttercream on the 10" sq drum. Place a layer centrally on the buttercream. Add 200g of buttercream then another layer.

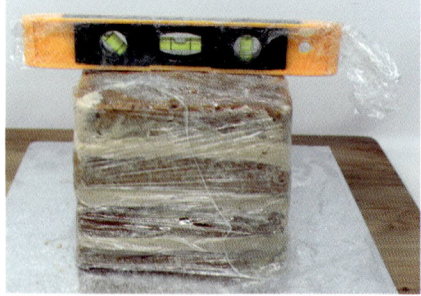

Repeat until you add the final layer upside down. Cling film, level and rest for four hours.

Ganaching the cake

Crumb coat the sides with a thin layer of ganache, paddling the ganache into any gaps and also to remove bubbles. Apply ganache to the top of the cake and smooth with a palette knife or royal icing ruler. Refrigerate for 15 minutes.

Apply another layer of ganache to the sides and top. Ensure that your scraper is vertical and use the scraper in a smooth motion to remove the excess from the sides of the cake. There is no need to neaten as we will add more ganache to fix the fence panels. Leave to set overnight.

Applying the ivy

Use a scribe to scratch the template where the leaves will go. Add texture with cocktail sticks.

Spread a small amount of ganache over the marked area.
Fix the leaves into place.

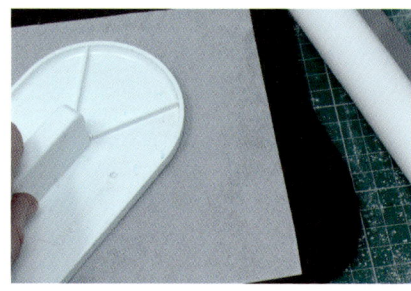

Fence Panels

Roll out chocolate sugarpaste to 5mm thick. Cut four pieces of the wafer paper to the same width as the cake and 1 inch taller, place on top of the paste and adhere with a smoother.

Brush the panels with a wide paint brush and water just enough to watch it change colour but not be soggy.
The wafer paper should only be slightly tacky to the touch but should not stick to your finger. (The paper to the left of the line has been wetted.)

Roll each panel vertically with a rolling pin, applying additional pressure and rolling back and fore in small movements to encourage the wafer paper to split in interesting ways resembling woodgrain. Cut the panels vertically into one inch wide panels.

Use a scalpel and ruler and cut 3/4" planks. Use the same template as for the fault line and cut again but slightly smaller on the sections that will be the front and front left sides.
Add splits and damage to the top and bottom edges.

Dust the panels with a mixture of dark cocoa powder, brown and black. Add pure black and green at the edges for interest.

Apply more ganache to the top and bottom of the fault line and apply those panels first.

Apply ganache to the rest of the cake and cover the sides.
Use a cake smoother to press against the panels to ensure they are firmly in place.

Spread a thin layer of ganache on the top of the cake and scatter a mixture of oreo and bourbon biscuit crumbs.

Roll out green sugarpaste to 3mm thick. Add texture by pressing the nailbrush firmly into the paste, twisting slightly while it is still in the paste.

Place the strips of paste to cover the board. Press the nailbrush over the joins. Cover the back with brown sugarpaste done the same way but overlap it with the green. Finish the board by dusting the grass with a mix of yellow at the edges, and green

Figure Modelling

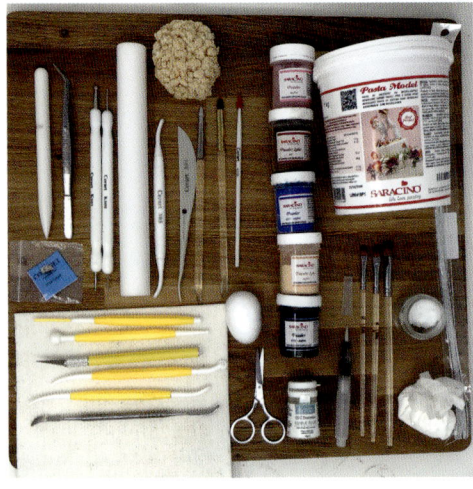

Ingredients

- Saracino modelling paste: white, grey
- SK Edible glue
- Saracino dusts: pink, brown, dark blue; skintone; black
- Coconut oil
- Cornflour puff
- 43g Rice krispie treats (recipe chapter 5)

Equipment

- Large celpin
- Angled tweezers
- Cerart ball tools
- Rolling pin
- Cerart 305
- Cerart 304
- Cerart No.2 soft taper
- Cerart No.2 round
- Cerart hard point
- 5cm poly egg
- PME scribe
- PME ball
- PME scalpel
- PME dresden
- PME stitch wheel
- Dekofee feather and hair tool
- Small scissors
- Glue brush
- Cerart filbert dusting Brushes
- Packet of 28g wires

Form 43g of Rice Krispie Treats into an oblong 7cms tall and 6cms wide at the top sloping to 5cms wide at the bottom.

Roll out 40g of skintone Saracino pasta model into 18cms wide by 11cms tall and wrap around and blend.

Roll 40g of skintone into a sausage shape and pinch the base flat as a mexican hat shape. Place over the shoulder area and blend down to make it smooth.

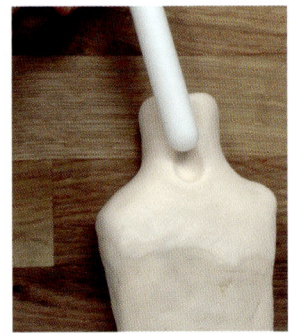

Press a large celpin into the neck and gently push down to hollow.

Use a number 4 round Cerart tool to draw around the Adam's apple.

Stroke the same tool down to mark the tendon then stroke across to the side.

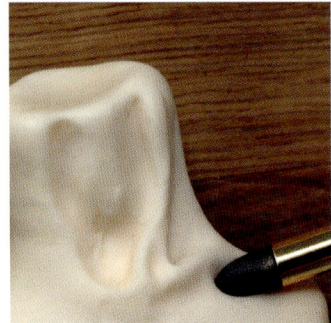

Stroke across under the tendon, and then push in firmly to create the hollow under the collar bone and in front of the shoulder.

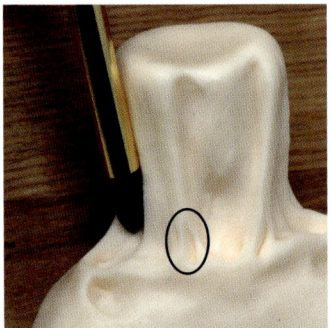

Mark additional tendons vertically in the neck, including a hollow at the base of the two inner tendons (as in the circle).

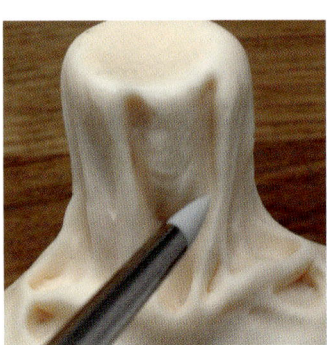

Use a No.2 soft taper tool to mark wrinkles and creases in the neck and across the adams apple.

Life Size Pic

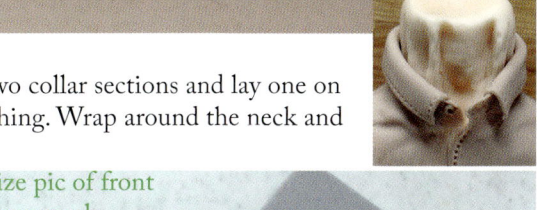

The Shirt Collar

Mix 1g of brown with 12g of white saracino and roll out the paste. Cut out the two collar sections and lay one on top of the other as in the image. Use a PME small stitch tool to mark in the stitching. Wrap around the neck and blend.

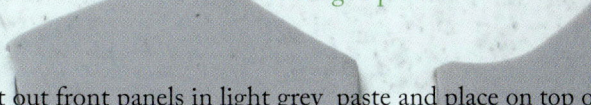

Life size pic of front cardigan panels

Cut out front panels in light grey paste and place on top of the dark grey. I used a micro oak leaf cutter but you can cut triangles. Emboss with the knitting mat. Fit the front sections one at a time onto the front of the figure, and use the mat to blend the joins.

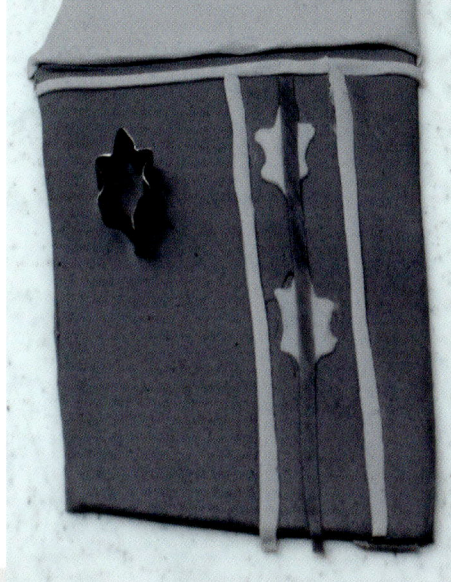

Cardigan

Colour 100g of white with 17g of black. Roll out and cut out the back panel using the front panel picture right as a guide. Press on the Knitting mat (above) to texture and trim to fit under the arm pits using a scalpel.

Life Size Pic
Arm Template

Make ribs for the zip cover and the neck by pressing strips with wires.

This is the textured front of the cardigan. Roll out strips and patterns thinly with this method so it doesn't distort the design.

Roll 26g of dark grey and make the left arm following the template and the right arm with 47g. Roll them in the mat and fix in place. Use a dresden to mark the folds.

Making Hands

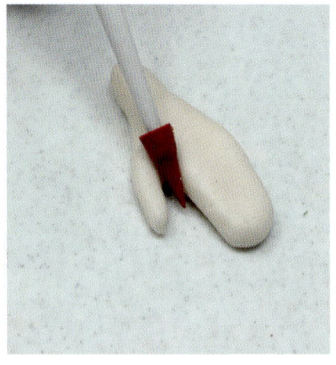

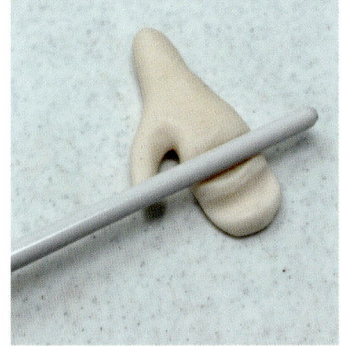

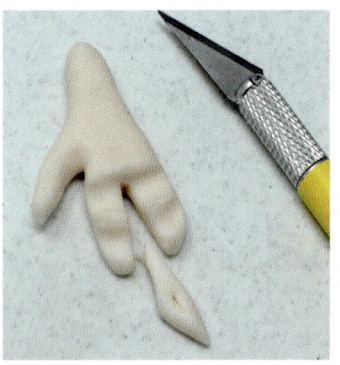

This pic is life size

Roll a 4.7g oval of skintone saracino. Twiddle the wrist area between finger and thumb. Thin the top of the hand then flatten the whole hand area. Remove a wedge 4/5ths across the hand with the scalpel so that it removes half of the thumb. Soften the gap with the hard point tool.

Press into the hand with the hard point handle after the knuckles and repeat to mark the joints, curving the angles to match the fingers. This means that you don't have to pinch in the knuckles and joints as they are already there. Remove another wedge in the centre.

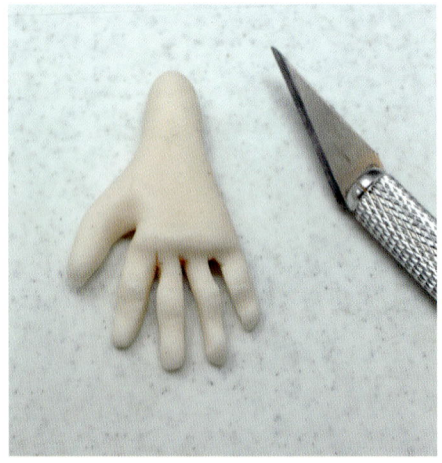

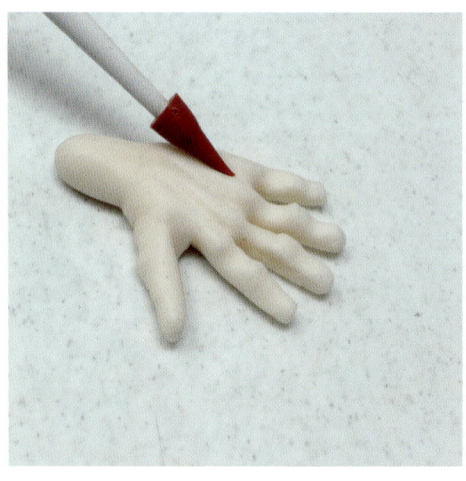

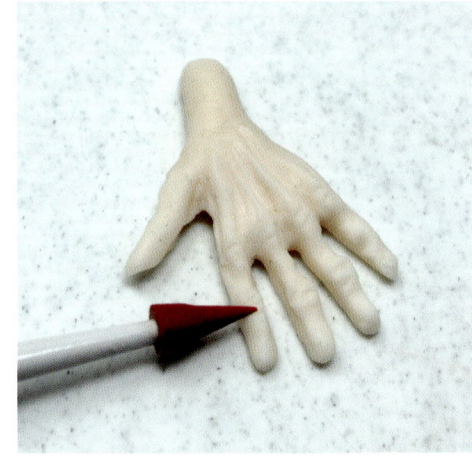

Soften all the edges then cut narrow wedges to divide the other fingers. Ensure they are cut to the correct lengths.

Insert the Cerart K2220 hard point tool between the fingers and gently lean back to create the webbing between the fingers and to shape the finger bones.

Mark the wrinkles in the joints.

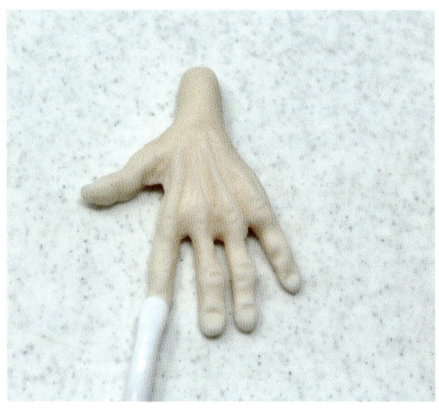

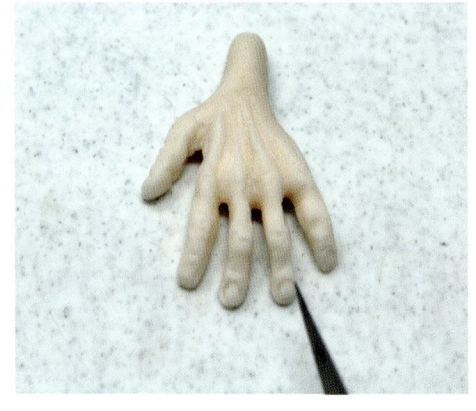

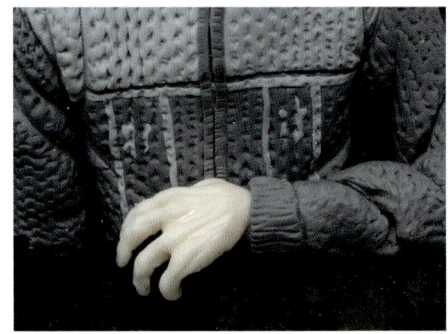

Press the small hand of the Cerart 305 tool to begin the nail embossing

Use the scalpel to mark down the side of the nail, and then to end the nail.

Push the hand into place in the hollow in the arm, and wrap another strip of the grey paste around for the cuff. Indent the lines with the back of the scalpel.

Making the Head

Flatten 70g of skintone saracino and wrap around a 5cm egg. Blend to seal. Push onto the kebab skewer.

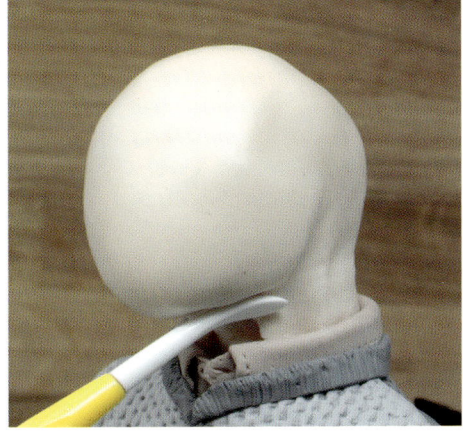

Blend with a dresden, emphasising the edge of the jaw at the back, but leaving the front loose.

Press either side of the temples with finger and thumb to indent.

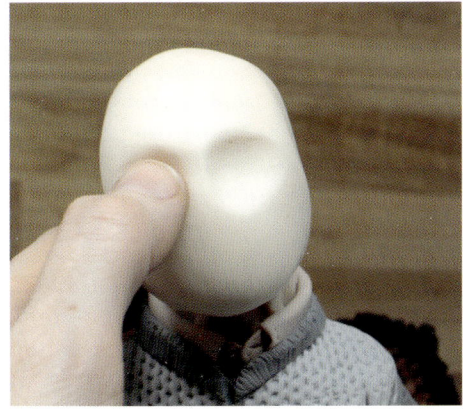

Push thumbs into the eye socket, only really pressing at the top. This is more a guide.

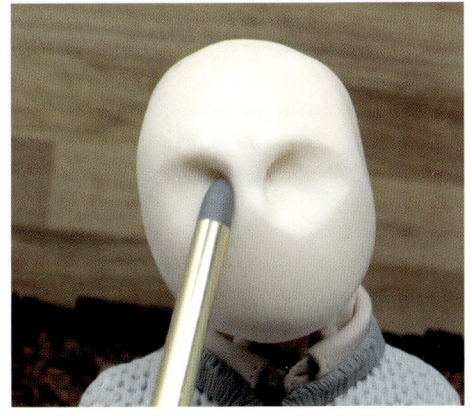

Use the No.4 Cerart round tool to indent further either side of the nose. Stroke down to shape the length.

Nose

End the nose, first by pressing in and up at the base of the nose, then neaten with the No.4 round.

Use the No.2 soft taper to heavily indent from above the nostril curve and curving around to follow the inside of the cheek.

Stroke from the outside of the nostril to tuck the nostril underneath. Careful not to crease the paste

Use a 2mm Cerart ball tool to push up and into the nostrils. Use the No.4 round to gently smooth around and down the nostril curve.

Gently soften the lower half of the cheek to soften the tool marks. You can also pull the smile lines wider now.

Mouth

Use the thumb to mark the shape of the cheek bones, and to press into the hollow of the cheeks.

Press the Cerart 304 blade to mark the line of the mouth and stroke up and down for the lips. Use the tip of the blade to neaten either side.

Stroke the No.4 round around the top edge of the upper lip to shape. Don't press hard so that it indents, just marks.

Use the No.2 soft taper to stroke down wrinkle lines at the corner of the mouth. Stroke the no.4 round from the edge of the lower lip and towards the middle.

Hollow under the lip, then add more wrinkles with the No.2 taper.

Eyes

Press the small end of the Cerart 305 upside down into the eye and move side to side to create the shape above.

Emphasise the crease of the upper eye lid with the hard point tool and add wrinkles. Don't be afraid to press hard.

Roll a double ended cone and cut in half lengthways. Insert into the eyes, using a soft brush to gently push them into place.

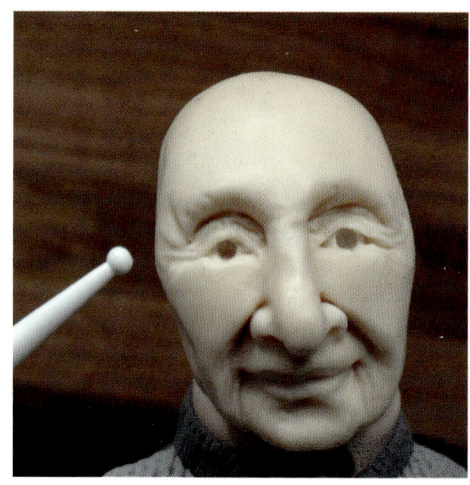

Use the PME small ball tool to push into the centre of the white. We will add the iris in later.

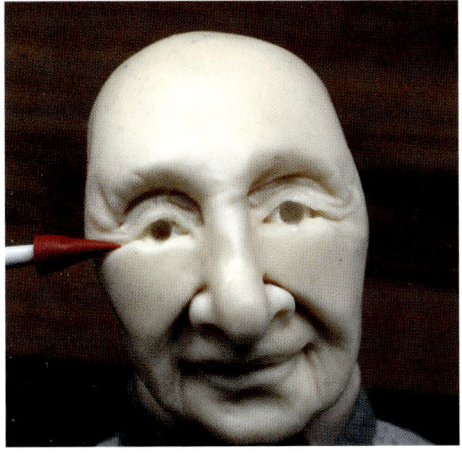

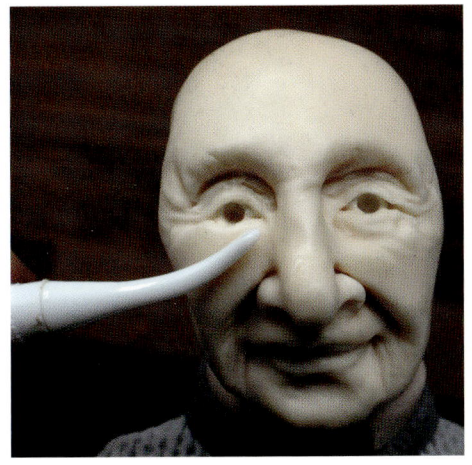

Emphasise the smile lines at the corner of the eyes with the hard point tool.
Be brave, it is the wrinkles that suggest the age.
Press the small end of the 305 firmly

to create the lower eye lid in the angle shown. Use the samel tool to end the eye lid in the outer corner and add gentle wrinkles.

Now you can have a little play and straighten up where needed. Remember the human face loosens with age, so won't necessarily appear symmetrical but that adds to the realism.

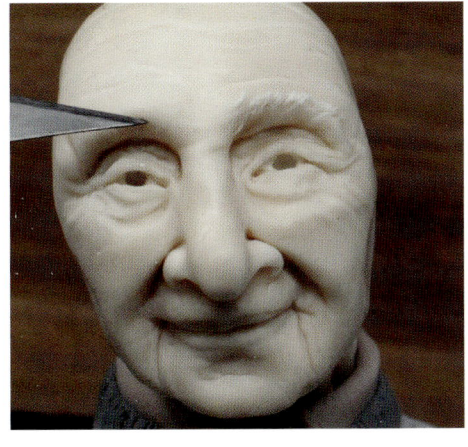

Scratch in eyebrows starting at the inner eyebrow using the PME scalpel.
Add more creases to the side of the cheek and forehead with the hard point tool.

I have put just the main parts of the ear rather than all of it.

This is what I concentrate on when making ears on small figures.

On life size busts you have to add as many details as possible for realism.

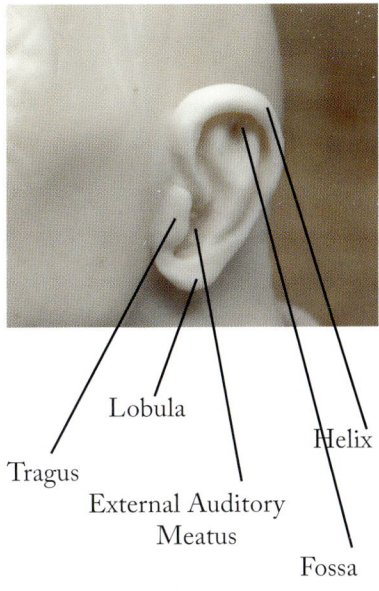

Lobula

Tragus

External Auditory Meatus

Helix

Fossa

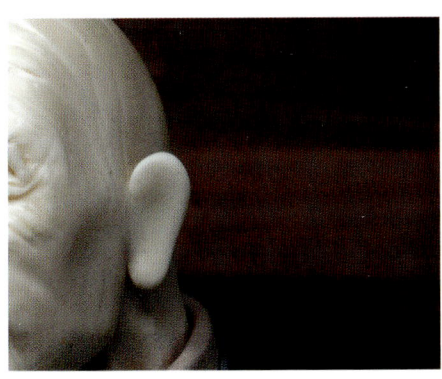

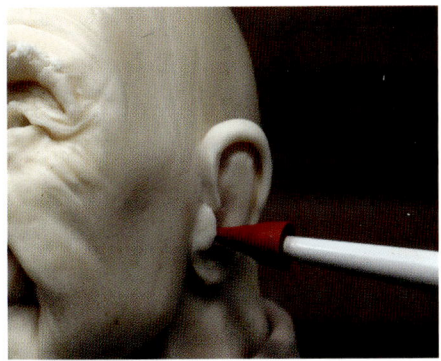

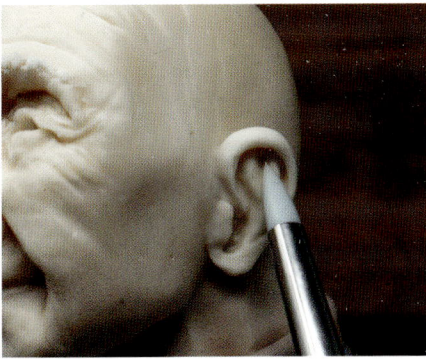

Roll 1.6g of skintone into a 1cm cone and cut in half vertically for the two ears. Soften the shape and press into place at the back of the chin. Pinch the Lobula between finger and thumb.

Use the No.2 soft taper to draw the helix shape around the outer ear, then use the hard point to draw another "C" for the tragus. Hollow the ear hole with the hard point and soften the shape.

Press the No.2 soft taper in the position shown to create the top of the fossa. Press around the ear with finger and thumb to make it more uneven. Add little creases in front of the tragus.

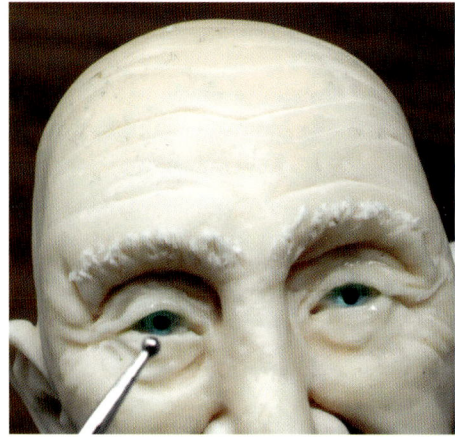

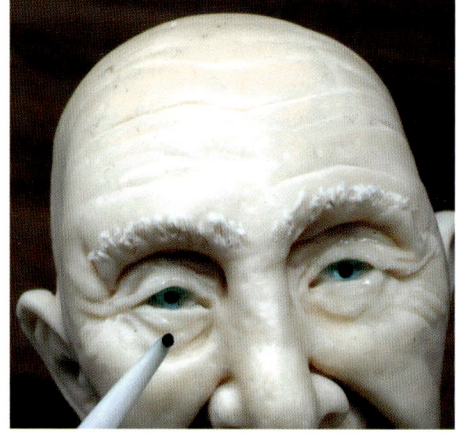

Looking to make a simpler figure?

Keep the neck smooth and shape mitten hands.

Start with a mould for the head and adjust the details to personalise.

Roll a tiny ball of Saracino blue modelling paste mixed with white and marbled and insert in for the iris.
Use the 1mm Cerart ball tool to hollow the very centre of the iris.

Use a glue brush to insert a really tiny ball of black in for the pupil.

Leave the eye to dry before painting.

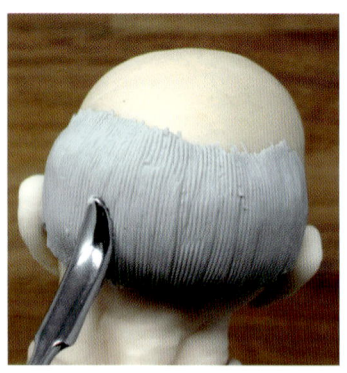

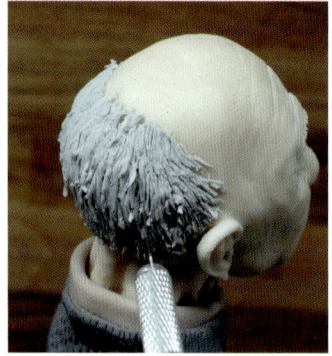

Hair

Roll 12g of pale grey into a strip and press into place at the back of the head. Note the neck markings.

Texture first with the Dekofee feather tool, then slash with a scalpel, feathering the hair about the ear and at the base.

To help add even more texture, snip with a small embroidery scissors. I slash through this with the scalpel again to remove too many

spikes.
Make sure the hair blends nicely into the forehead using the scalpel, careful not to mark any lines on the head.

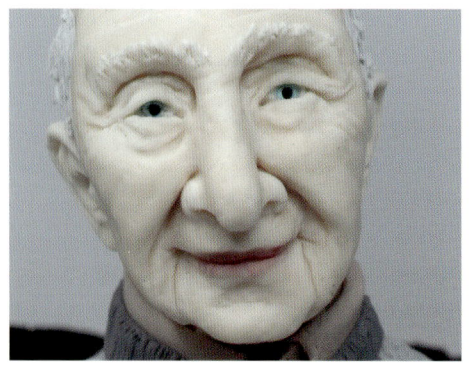

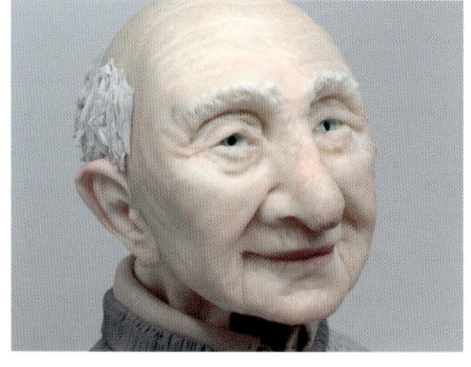

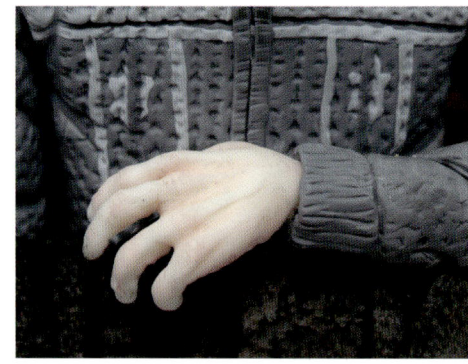

Colouring

Dust Saracino pink onto the lips with a No.4 filbert brush and only dusting the cut line at the centre of the lips and dusting side to side. The overdust will automatically colour the rest of the lips.

Use the same pink colour to add to the eyebrow, nose, front of cheeks, crease of the chin and the base of the chin, across the forehead and .or the eyes, dust the bags under the eye and the outer corner of the eye.

Dust the same pink onto the knuckles and joints of the fingers and inbetween the bones on the back of the hand.

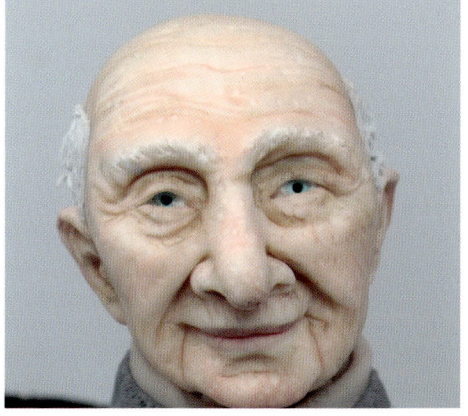

Mix Saracino brown with the pink, and begin to add depth inside the ear, at the side of the nose both around the nostrils, inside them and the inner eye. Also the wrinkles on the face.

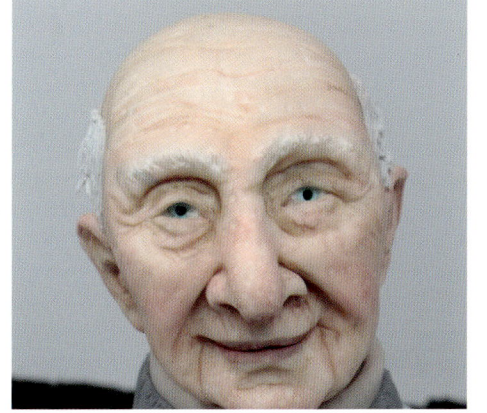

Now be bold and add neat pink to emphasise the pink on the nose and cheeks and neat brown into the wrinkles, especially the deeper areas. Dust the hollows on the neck and in between the fingers.

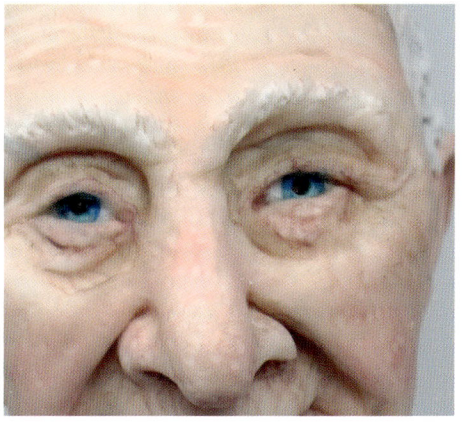

Mix Saracino blue dust with dipping solution, not too thick, and start at the top of the iris, brushing the paint down the side with a Sugar Press detail brush.

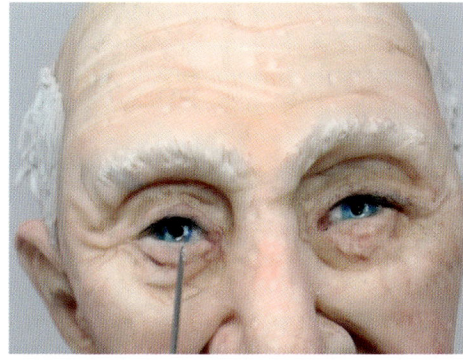

Use a scribe to add white to the iris around the black pupil.
Use the same white to add white to the tips of the nails on the hand.

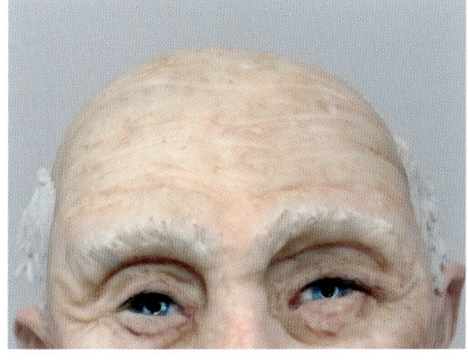

Heavily dilute brown and pink together and paint very washy stippled age spots on the forehead and on the cheeks.

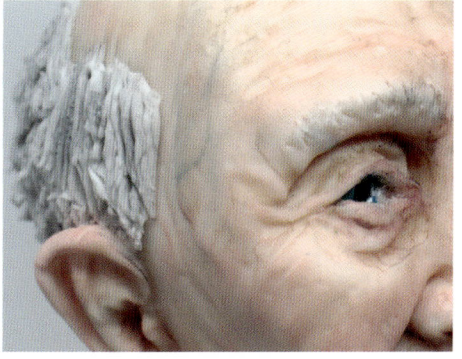

Dust black onto the hair and eyebrows with a fine brush, dusting only the lines and not the surface. Dilute blue with dipping solution and paint very fine veins on the temples.

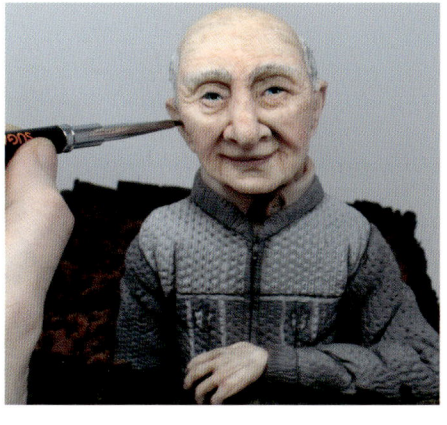

Dust the clothing by emphasising the shading using the same black for the creases in the cardigan and in the hollows at the wrist of the cardigan. Add more depth to the very centre of the ear hole

Complete the cake by adding broken up pieces of the Honey Cake Moss using the recipe in chapter 2. Placing so that the rough sides are up.
Fix the ribbon around the cake drum with double sided tape.

Using posy pics, insert the rose stem into the bottom right hand side of the cake, and the ivy coming out of the fault.

7

Rusty

Cyril took a deep breath and climbed right to the top of the fence .....but wait!
What was that! He jumped in shock.

"OH NO!" shouted Cyril "That's a fox!"

He was just about to jump straight back down and run all the way home,
when Mr Morris said

"Oh! but that is just old Rusty the Fox, fast asleep in my vegetable patch.
He likes sleeping among the potatoes best!" chuckled Mr Morris.

"But what should I do!" said Cyril, now very anxious.

"Well, if you creep past him nice and quietly" said Mr Morris,
"then I think you will do just fine."

Cyril very carefully crept past old Rusty until he reached the spring green grass dotted with daisies, and he ran, and he ran, and he ran.

How fast can you run?

He stopped, a little out of breath, and looked back just in time to see Rusty pouncing on a crunchy brown leaf.

"Phew! THAT was close!" he said, and he started walking towards the pond.

Rusty the Fox

Perfect for cupcakes, but if you are short of time, you could always use the mould by FPC Sugarcraft.

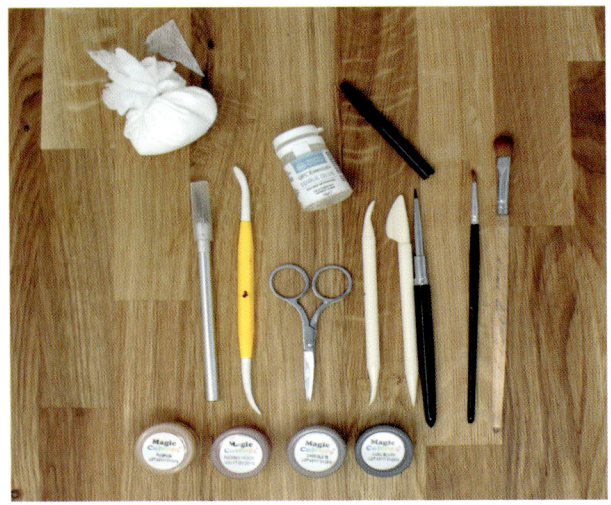

Ingredients

- 53g White Saracino Pasta Model
- Magic colours: Pumpkin: Riding Hood, Chocolate, Coal Black
- PME Spray Glaze
- Edible Glue

This is an actual size template for sleepy Rusty

Equipment

- Small Sharp Scissors
- Scalpel with No.11 blade
- Sugarpress Brush 1
- Cerart no.8 filbert
- brush
- FMM Cone Tool
- PME Dresden
- FMM Dresden
- Glue Brush

Roll Saracino into the above shapes tail 8.3g, hind legs x 2 3.5g front legs x 2 2.1g and body 31g Check the sizes against the Rusty template above.

Cut 2cms off the front of the head area, and fix the legs into position as in the picture Saracino does not need glue to fix as long as it is still soft.

Texture the body with a scalpel, starting from the head area and down the back.

Ensure to texture the fur down the legs.

Shape the head from 12g of paste and press into place on the neck area. Use a scalpel to mark the eyes and mouth area as shown.

Texture the head as before. Carefully mark the fur from the nose and towards the back of the head. Use a scissors to snip additional fur on the cheek.

Shape the ears from 0.8g each of Saracino. Roll to a teardrop. Press the PME dresden into the ear as shown in the image, then pinch the tip to a point.

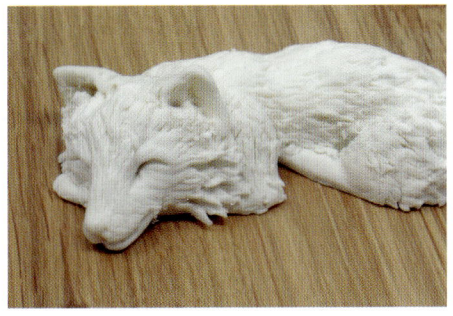

Press the ears into place on the head. If the head is too dry, use edible glue sparingly to fix.

Re#knead the tail to ensure that it is soft, then create a hollow with the FMM cone tool. Insert the tail into the body and texture down its length with the scalpel.

Snip additional texture into the tail with the small sharp scissors.

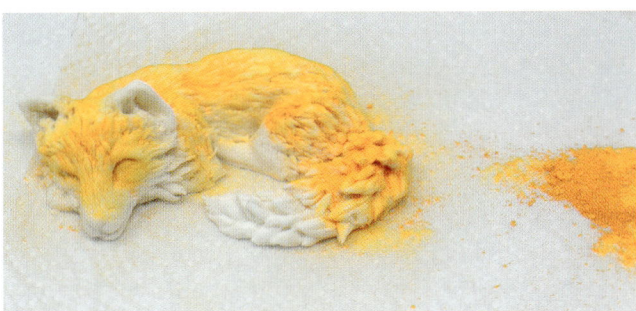

Begin to dust the fox with a No.8 filbert brush using the Magic Colours Pumpkin Dust. Leave the ears, legs, muzzle, cheeks and tail white.

Mix the Pumpkin with Riding hood and lightly over dust. Next mix the pumpkin and Riding Hood mix with the Chocolate and add depth, especially around shoulders and behind the head.

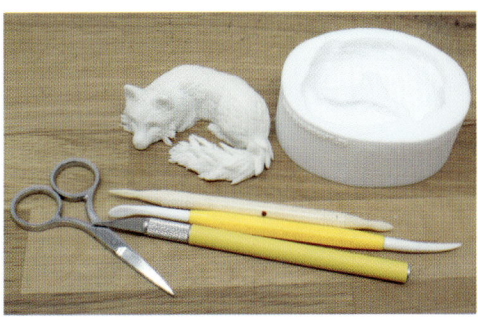

I worked with the wonderful FPC Sugarcraft and they created a Rusty mould which is perfect for cupcakes. I snip the tail and cheeks with scissors and hollow the ears with a dresden to complete the design.

Using coal black and the same brush, first dust onto the tips and backs of the ears, the legs and lightly dust the tail. Finally, use the Sugar Press No.1 brush and dust into the eye, on the nose and into the mouth.

Squeak the Mouse

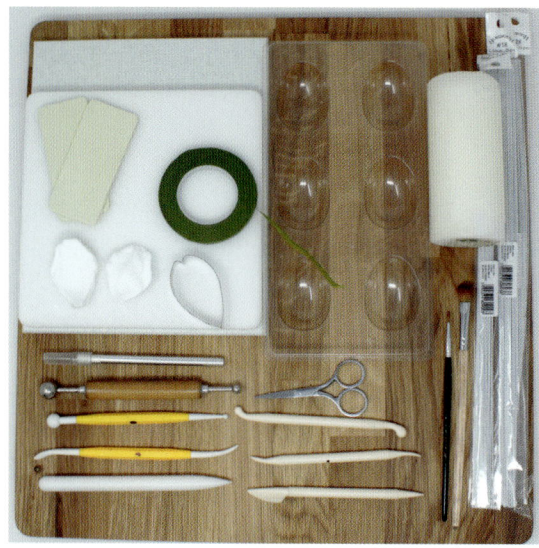

Ingredients

- 65g SK flowerpaste
- SK sunflower dust
- SK white dust
- SK leaf green dust
- SK holly/ivy green dust
- SK chestnut dust
- SK bulrush dust
- SK damson dust
- SK fuschia dust
- 2 x 4mm black dragees
- PME Spray Glaze
- Edible Glue
- Cornflour

Equipment

- Celboard
- Celpad
- Scalpel
- PME & metal ball tools
- FMM bone tools
- PME & FMM dresdens
- Celpin large
- FMM cone tool
- Embroidery scissors
- Tulip cutter
- SK parrot tulip veiner
- Easter egg mould
- Sugar City corn husk veiner
- Dusting Brushes
- 18, 20, 26g white florist wire
- Nile green florist tape

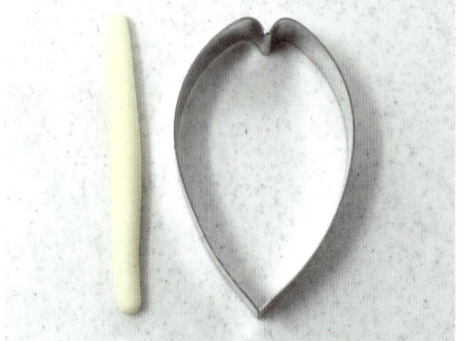

Roll a sausage of flowerpaste coloured with SK sunflower dust colour into a 0.5cm wide sausage the length of the tulip petal cutter.

Create a ridge in the centre of the paste by pressing the celpin down onto the paste and rolling to the right, then pressing on the centre and rolling to the left. Repeat until you achieve the thickness of ridge suitable for the 26g white wire.

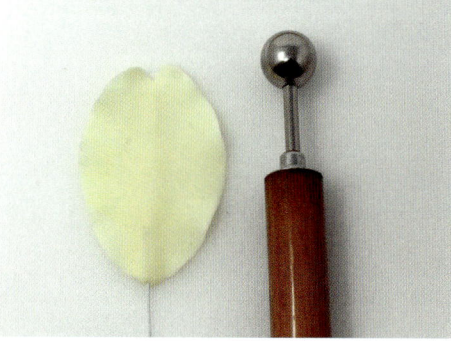

Dip a half length 26g white wire in edible glue and wipe off the excess. Insert one third into the wire. Place the petal on a foam pad and thin the edges by drawing the large metal ball tool half on and half off the edge of the petals.

Place the wired petal face up in the female or recessed side of the tulip petal veiner. Hold the wire to keep in place and carefully line up the veiners and press firmly.

Place the petal right way up on the foam pad and use the FMM dresden to shape the tip of the petal, by dragging down from the tip 1cm down repeatedly.

Place the petal into an easter egg mould to dry.
Pushing the petal into shape and curling the tip further forward.

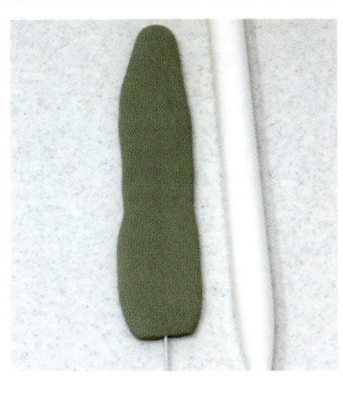

Use 14g Squires Kitchen Holly/Ivy flowerpaste Roll into a sausage, flatten with your hand and insert a 20g wire.

Use the Celpin and create a ridge up the length of the leaf in the same manner as with the petal shape.

Glue and insert the wire almost to the tip of the leaf for support. Cut the leaf shape with a scalpel on your workboard. Place the leaf on a celpad and thin the edges with a ball tool as before, before veining with the Sugar City Corn husk veiner. Gently shape the leaf pulling the tip back and pulling the sides forward.

Leather dry is when the surface of the paste has begun to set, but underneath is still pliable.

Dust the leaf with SK leaf green, then in the centre and base of the leaf with SK holly/ivy before adding a little SK damson to the tip.

Fix the colours on the leaf by lightly spraying with PME spray glaze. Allow to dry then add a second coat. Allow the leaf to dry until leather dry then shape the leaf slightly around the stem.

Dust the petals from base to tip, leaving the sides lighter than the rest. On the back of the petal, leave patches slightly lighter by dusting streaks downward.

Roll 20g white SK flowerpaste into the above shape and size. Stand the shape on the wide end.
(Pic above is actual size.)

Bend the head shape so that it comes forward. Create the muzzle by rolling the side of the PME dresden tool either side as in the picture.

Create hollows for the ears using the FMM cone tool.

Indent the eye sockets for the mouse using the small ball on the PME ball tool.

Gently inert the two 4mm black dragees. Treat the mouse nose as the centre of a clock, and use a scalpel to scratch fur moving away from the clock centre.

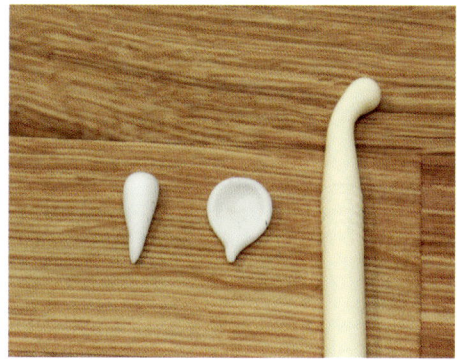

Take 0.7g of white SK flowerpaste and divide into two for the ears. Roll into a cone shape. Press the small side of the FMM bone tool to create the hollow of the ear. Pinch the base to narrow.

Paint a small amount of glue inside the holes for the ears and wait 30 seconds for the glue to become tacky.
Gently push the ears into place.

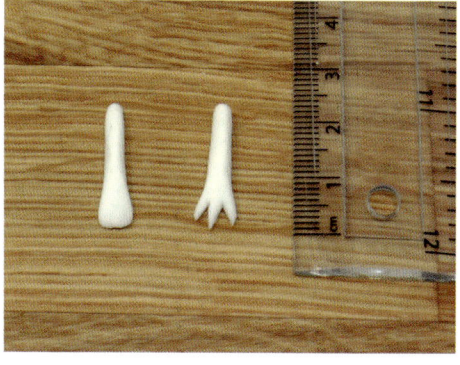

Divide 1.4g of SK white flowerpaste into four for the legs.
Roll each piece into 2cm long sausages and gently press your finger to flatten one end of each.
Cut two small V shapes out of each foot and soften the shapes.

Cup the hands gently to leave space for the tail to fit into.
Push the FMM cone tool into the body and paint a small amount of glue into the holes with a paintbrush.
Fix the front arms into place. You can also glue them together.

Cut the two back legs 0.5cm shorter. Push two more holes into the body with the FMM cone tool and glue the feet into place. Twist 0.8g SK white flowe paste onto a 7cm length of 26g wire.

Create a hollow with the FMM cone tool for the tail, glue inside and insert the wire of the tail. Coil the tail around the body and push the tip of the tail into the paws. You can move this to dust the paws, nose

and ears with a SK fuschia and SK white dust mix.
Dust the body and back of the ears with chestnut.

Dust dark patches on the body and the tips of the ears with SK bulrush. Dust a little inside the mouth.
Spray with PME spray glaze to set the colours.

Bend a hook on the end of an 18g white wire and hold in the flame of a candle for 10 seconds. Be careful not to touch the hot wire.

Push the hot wire straight away into the base of the mouse at least 3/4 of the way up and don't move for 20 seconds to allow it to cool. There will be a little smoke and candy smell.

Take half width nile green florist tape and begin to tape the petals around the mouse.

Tape three petals around the mouse first, then add the other three as a second row in the gaps between the previous row.

Tape down to the bottom, then wrap 1 inch wide strips of kitchen paper around the stem of the tulip twice to thicken.

Tape the stem with full width florist tape tightly twice, then run the blade of the scissors up and down to remove the tape marks.

Tape in the leaf and wrap the base of the leaf around the stem, thicken as before. Dust the stem with leaf green and holly/ivy to finish.

Vegan Brownie Cupcakes

These are a firm favourite in our house, so I just had to share the recipe.

Ingredients

- 250g plain flour
- 375g demerara sugar
- 80g cocoa powder
- 1 tsp baking powder
- 1 tsp salt
- 1 tsp vanilla extract
- 1 tbsp coffee granules mixed in 2 tbsp hazelnut milk
- 300ml hazelnut milk
- 200ml vegetable oil

Additions:
- 70g chopped walnuts
- 70g small chopped dark choc

Equipment

- Large bowl and mixer with K beater or a wooden spoon
- Muffin cases
- Muffin tin

Vegan Ganache

Gently melt 300g of Vegan dark chocolate. Warm coconut cream and stir in 1tbsp. It will thicken straight away. If you want it thinner for pouring, add 1-2 tbsp more and stir until blended.

Not decorating the cupcakes but just making them for something tasty to eat?

Try adding extra walnut and chopped chocolate sprinkled on top before you pop them in the oven, then lightly dust with icing sugar through a sieve when they are cool. Delicious!

Method: Makes 12

1. Preheat the oven to 180 C / Gas mark 4.
2. Put all ingredients except the additions into your mixing bowl, and mix using a Kenwood K beater or a wooden spoon.
3. When mixed, gently stir in the chopped walnuts and chopped dark chocolate.
4. Use an ice cream scoop to fill your cupcake cases.
5. Bake for 30 to 40 minutes on the centre shelf of the oven (30 mins if you want gooey brownie middles).
6. Remove from the oven when the top surface of the brownies have changed to a matt finish.
7. Allow to cool in the cupcake tin.

Storage
8. Store in a cake tin lined with greaseproof paper for up to one week but they also freeze really well.

Want another option? Try swapping the walnuts and coffee milk for pecans and maple syrup.

These cupcakes are a perfect way to put all your favourite things in there....

Vegetable Cupcakes

Who can resist miniature vegetables, I know I can't.

Ingredients

- Saracino Pasta model: white, light green
- Squires Kitchen dust colours: Berberis, dark green
- Sugarflair Paste: Autumn Leaf
- Sugarflair Dust: Nutkin Brown
- Cornflour
- Edible Glue
- Peanut butter

Equipment

- Flat Cutting Blade
- PME Dresden
- FMM Cone tool
- Cearart No.2 taper tool
- Celpin
- Scalpel
- Sharp knife
- Squires Kitchen GI savoy cabbage veiner
- Nail brush
- Work board

Covering the Cupcake

Spread the 1 tbsp of softened peanut butter over the cupcake. Roll out 25g of Renshaws chocolate brown sugarpaste and texture using the nailbrush by firmly pushing the nailbrush into the paste while twisting a little. Cut out using the 7cm circle cutter and fit in place on top of the cupcake.

Potatoes

Colour Saracino pasta model with Sugarflair Autumn leaf. Roll into uneven ball and oval shapes. Roll in Sugarflair nutkin brown dust to add dirt.

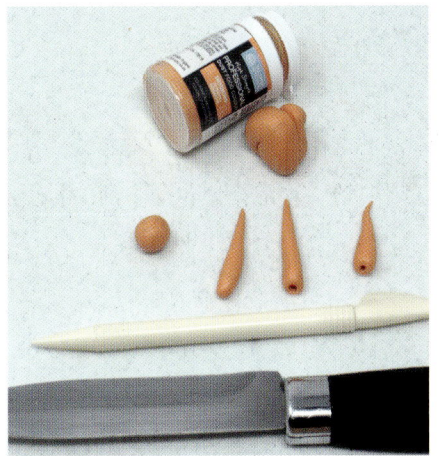

Carrots

Roll a 1g ball of Berberis Saracino. Roll to a 2cm tapered cone. Push the cone tool in the wide end and mark with the knfe.

Roll a 1g ball of dark green saracino into a cone and flatten.
Drag the PME veining tool to cut the paste, pinch and push in place.

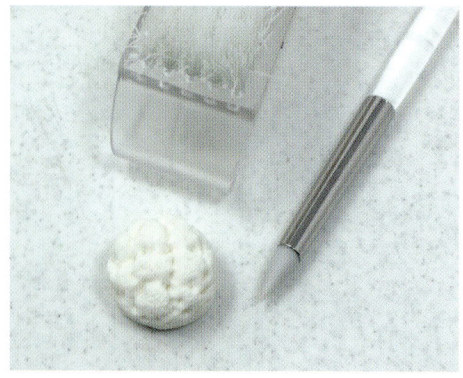

Cauliflower
Roll a 5g ball of white saracino. Texture with a nailbrush then draw circles using the Cerart no.2 taper tool.

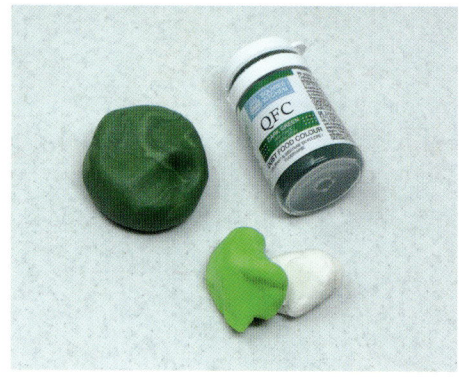

Mix 5g white and light green with a little dark green dust. Colour 23g light green with dark green dust.

To make a cane for the leaves, Flatten the 23g ball and cut in half. Roll out the lighter colour and cut into the pieces shown in the picture above.

Cut the dark green circle into slices as shown, add a vein shape in the centre, and thinner pieces in the others.

Cut triangles out of the ends of veins and wrap thinner pieces around the wedges before replacing them.
Add as many of the wedges as you wish for more detail.

Compress the shape so that the pattern becomes smaller and more of a sausage shape.

Cut slices, flatten and then vein in the cabbage veiner.

(Store your spare cane wrapped in cling film and in a sandwich bag.

Wrap five leaves around the centre shape, overlapping.
As long as the leaves are not dry, you won't need any edible glue to fix them.

Then add a second row of 5-6 leaves. Bend and twist them a little for extra texture.

Assembling the Scene

Making your cake two sided means you can hide fabulous details on the back, so if you pop the cake on a turntable, you have the element of surprise.

Ingredients

- Rolling pin
- Nail brush
- Palette knife
- Large ball tool
- Large PME scribe
- Piping bag
- Tweezers

Equipment

- Renshaws Chocolate brown sugarpaste
- Renshaws green sugarpaste

Cover the board area with 180g chocolate brown sugarpaste. Fix in place with water. Texture with a nailbrush as for the cupcakes. Pinch grass texture with a tweezers.

Cover a cupcake as in chapter 4. Indent where you wish Rusty to lie on the cupcake by gently indenting with a large ball tool, moisten the sugarpaste and sit Rusty on top.

Indent where the cabbage will go and fix the cauliflower in place with a little water. Press the carrots and potatoes into place.

Use a large PME scribe tool or an Awl to push a hole into the cake drum for the flower stem to sit into. Pipe a little brown sugarpaste gunge into the hole then cover with brown sugarpaste.

Place the two cupcakes onto the board on the left hand side. Push brown sugarpaste around them and texture with a nailbrush. Add extra vegetables into the earth and honey cake moss on the board to finish.

8

The Pond

"Oh! how lovely!" exclaimed Cyril.
The sound of the water burbling away as it jumped off the stones was music to his ears
after so much running. "Perhaps I will just have a little rest here."

He sat down on a marble stone that was all toasty and warm in the sun and leaned back to rest.
Popping his arms behind his head he said to himself "How lovely!" and closed his eyes.
It was so peaceful here by the water, he could even hear the whirring of Dewi the dragonfly's'
wings as he flew from bulrush to bulrush.

Cyril was SO comfortable, and SO happy lying in the sun, that soon he fell quite fast asleep!

"Hum-Hum! Excuse me! That's my stone you have there!" piped up a very small voice,
obviously trying to make themselves sound much bigger than they really were.

Cyril scrambled up to his feet. "Oh my! Oh no! I am so very sorry!"
and he jumped off the stone.

"That's quite alright" said the turtle in a much gentler voice and
gave a big smile to Cyril
before taking a HUGE bite out of a leaf.

"You have to be careful you know, anyone could hop over
the fence, but......you seem quite nice"

COUGH COUGH!
Then in a much tinier voice said, "I'm Ree Ree.
Pleased to meet you."
Ree Ree was a small green turtle with a big grin.

"Hello Ree Ree, I'm Cyril. I don't suppose you could help
me get across this pond could you?
I am trying to meet Luna the cat who lives in the cottage."

"Hop onto my back" said Ree Ree "and I will swim across so that you
don't get wet."

Cyril hopped quite carefully onto Ree Ree's back and she started swimming
to the other side of the pond.
"You are nearly there now" said Ree Ree, "The house is just past that
cow parsley"
"Oh thank you Ree Ree, it was so nice to meet you" and Cyril ran off waving his
little paw.

Dewi Dragonfly

Ingredients

- Rainbow Dust: black magic, royal blue, sunset yellow, irridescent green fusion
- Culpitt dipping solution
- 1g SK flowerpaste
- 1 tsp gelatine

Equipment

- Sugarcity dragonfly mould 4cm
- 24g wire
- Global Sugar artist master series 00 brush
- palette
- Cake Connection dragonfly veining sheet
- PME dresden

Bloom 1 tsp of gelatin powder in 2 1/2 tsp water. Melt in the microwave gently for 10 second intervals until dissolved. Sprinkle Rainbow Dust irridescent green fusion and paint over the veining sheet. Leave to dry until it frees itself from the sheet.

Push 1g of SK flowerpaste into the dragonfly mould dusted with cornflour. Use a dreden tool to push the paste into the smaller areas.
Carefully remove.

Paint the body with a mixture of sunset yellow, royal blue and black magic mixed with Culpitt dipping solution and using a Global Sugar Artist Network master series 00 brush.

Insert a hooked 24g white wire into the underside of the dragonfly body.

The dragonfly can also be all moulded from flowerpaste.

Leave the wings white and add the tiny black dots.

Cut out the wings with a scissors. Paint a small amount of piping gel onto the upper body and gently press the wings into place.

Bulrushes

I will admit that the pond cake design was just an excuse to create a bulrush.
I think they are such a dramatic plant.

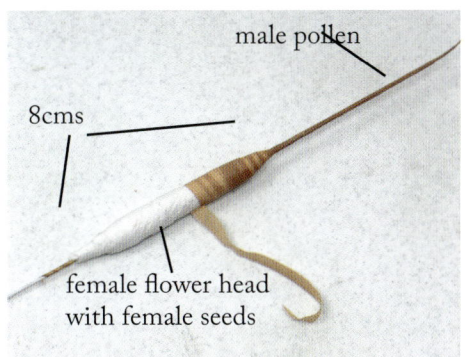

Ingredients

- Ground almonds
- Edible glue
- 21g SK flower paste
- SK dusts: sunflower, chestnut, bulrush, leaf green, dark green
- PME piping gel

Equipment

- White wires: 18g, 24g
- Floral tape: beige, nile green
- no.8 filbert brush
- Kitchen paper
- Strong scissors

8cms

male pollen

female flower head with female seeds

Tape over the top half of an 18g wire five times with half width beige tape. Cut kitchen paper into 3cm wide strips and wrap around an 8cm section 10cm down from the top with the paper. Tape over this flower head three times and add a twisted section of tape just above it.

Mix SK chestnut and bulrush with the ground almonds which will represent the female seeds.
Paint the taped section with piping gel then roll in the almond mix to cover the female flower head.

Stretch a 70cm length of full width nile green tape. Place a 24g wire on and fold over the tape to cover the wire. Trim the top to a point with the scissors. (as the instructions on p.40). Crumple the point to look like a damaged leaf.

Dust the tip of the leaves and just under the flower head with sunflower. Dust the rest of the leaf with leaf green mixed with dark green, then dust the tips of the leaves with bulrush. Dust under the flower head with chestnut and just above with bulrush. Tape the dusted leaves in place, wrapping each around the stem.

Ree Ree the Turtle

Little Ree Ree the Turtle was a demonstration subject that I later gave to lovely Mary. Her Mum Breda told me later that Mary had named her Ree Ree, so Ree Ree she is.

Ingredients

- 100g Saracino pasta model
- Magic Colours airbrush: yellow, light green, dark green
- Kroma green airbrush colour
- 4mm black dragees
- Culpitt dipping solution
- Edible glue
- Cornflour puff
- PME spray glaze

Equipment

- Pliers
- Rolling pin
- Small sharp knife
- PME small ball tool
- PME dresden
- Cerart No.2 taper soft
- Kemper coarse fur texture tool
- Glue brush
- Dust brushes & palette
- Non slip mat
- Cling film
- Tweezers
- Cerart K2220 hard point
- Scalpel
- 18g, 24g white wire
- white florist tape

Bend the 18g wire for a 1cm head and a 2cm neck, then a 2" circle and bend down one leg. Add additional lengths of 18g wire for the other side of the circle and down another leg, then add a piece across the body and down the other two legs. Twist the 24g wire to secure and tape in place with white florist tape. Cover the body area with white florist tape.

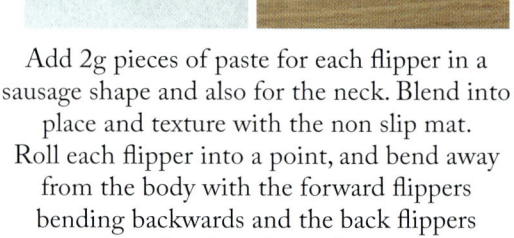

Pin out 47g white Saracino to 2mm thick and a 6" circle.

Place the turtle on top and pull paste up and over the body. Join over the top and blend together to fix.

Texture all of the paste with non slip matting, pressing firmly.

Add 2g pieces of paste for each flipper in a sausage shape and also for the neck. Blend into place and texture with the non slip mat. Roll each flipper into a point, and bend away from the body with the forward flippers bending backwards and the back flippers bending forward.

Roll a 2" 14g long oval of Saracino 2mm thick. Mark the underbelly details with the No.2 soft taper Cerart tool and texture with scrunched cling film. Add a tiny triangle tail. Press the under shell in place, ensuring you do not blend into the body. Create a slight hollowed groove down the belly from hand to tail.

Form a slightly larger 25g oval with a central ridge down its length. Use the PME veining tool to create the markings. Fix in place on the turtles back.

Roll 2g of Saracino for the head and blend onto the neck. Make the head slightly pointed at the snout and with a slight ridge on the top of the head.

Push a 2mm ball tool in for the eye and hook out the eyelid by pulling the ball tool slightly up and out pulling the paste. Use the hard point tool to push in two nostrils.

Cut open the mouth with a scalpel and open with the dresden by pushing in and pulling down.
Gently push the lower jaw back in so that it sits under the upper jaw.

Push two 4mm black dragees in for eyes and emphasise the upper and lower lids by rolling the veining tool over the eye lid.

Colouring
Airbrush Magic Colours yellow over the turtle. Leave the underbelly quite clean.

Mix Magic Colours yellow and light green airbrush colour and colour the turtle in a patchy way, leaving some yellow areas clean.

Airbrush with Kroma green, particularly in the lines and the edge of the shell. Use a piece of kitchen paper and dab at the shell.

Add depth with Magic Colours dark green then spray just the shell with PME spray glaze.

Vegan Banana Cake

Banana loaf was a staple for after school snacks when the boys were small, so a banana cake was a natural choice for one of the recipes. I must confess to stealing a slice as not the whole loaf is needed.

Ingredients

- 4 bananas 350g
- 70g Stork Block
- 100g soft brown sugar
- 250g SR flour
- 1 tsp baking powder
- 1 tsp vanilla extract
- 75ml Soya milk
- 50g chopped hazelnuts
- 70g sultanas

Equipment

- 2 lb loaf tin
- Large mixing bowl
- Wooden spoon
- Scissors
- Greaseproof Paper

Method

1. Pre heat the oven to 170 C/Gas 3.
2. Line a 2lb loaf tin by greasing with vegan spread and lining with greaseproof paper.
3. Cream the block margarine, then add the bananas and mix well.
4. Add the sugar to the bowl and mix again.
5. Add the sieved self raising flour and the baking powder and fold into the mix.
6. Stir in the milk.
7. Stir in the vanilla extract.
8. Finally, add in the sultanas and the hazelnuts, folding
9. carefully.
10.
11. Bake for 45 minutes then insert a skewer. If the skewer does not come out clean, Cover the surface with a piece of foil and return to the oven for 15 minutres.
12. Cool in the tin on a cooling rack for 5 minutes, then place the rack on top of the tin and invert. Leave for a further 10 minutes then turn out and cool on the baking rack.

To make the cake easier to remove from the tin, place greaseproof paper on top of the tin and cut out a square at each corner.
The greaseproof should be large enough to cover both the base and up the sides.

Pond Cake

I don't use Isomalt very often, but I think it doesn't matter if you have never worked with Isomalt before, the pre-cooked tiles make it accessible to everyone.
I don't include it as an edible part of the cake, but as a removable decoration as it is very sharp and can be brittle, so I don't tend to use it for children's cakes.

Ingredients
- 2 banana loaf cakes
- 200g peanut butter
- 2 tbsp coconut cream
- 600g dark chocolate
- 750g Renshaw decorice sugarpaste
- Magic Colours black airbrush colour
- Kroma green airbrush colour
- Honey cake moss
- Sugarflair shadow grey gel

Equipment
- Sharp knife
- Palette knife
- Aluminium foil
- 6" round cake card
- Clairella Cakes airbrush
- Spectrum Flow shell and shine
- Nailbrush

Cut the crust off each of the banana loaf cakes. Spread the peanut butter onto the cake card. Fix the first layer of cake on and spread the rest of the peanut butter.

Carve the edges off the cake to soften the shape.

Melt 600g dark chocolate in the microwave for 30 seconds. Stir, then melt for another 30 seconds. Stir, then melt in 10 seconds bursts until 2/3rds of the chocolate is melted, stir until smooth.

Warm the coconut cream. Add 1 tbsp to the melted chocolate and stir quickly. If the chocolate is still too thick, stir in 1 tbsp of hot water which will thin the ganache down again.

You can also make the vegan ganache with just chocolate and a little hot water. Spread the ganache onto the cake straight away and refrigerate for 30 minutes to set.

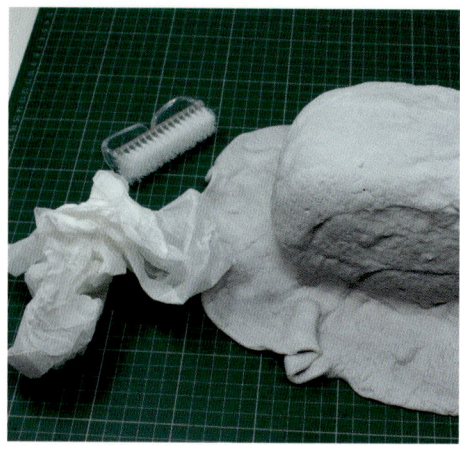

Roll out 450g white sugarpaste coloured with shadow grey. While rolled out, texture with scrunched greaseproof and a nailbrush. Cover the cake without using a smoother and trim the excess.

Scrunch foil tightly and open back out. Place over the cake and pinch shape and texture with finger and thumb through the foil.

Work to create multiple ledges that the water can drip off.
Using the remaining 300g grey sugarpaste, create little rocks and leave to dry.

Colour the rock by airbrushing with Magic Colours black colour. Brush in one direction so that it creates shadows and light patches. Add depth at the base and a little Kroma green on the side that will face the pond.

Airbrush the front of the large rock that will touch the pond with Kroma green. Wait until dry and then spray with Spectrum flow Shell and shine to give the impression of being wet.

Use a scalpel to create a hole wide enough for the bulrush stem to sit in.
Pipe sugarpaste mixed with edible glue into the hole and push in the bulrush.
Cover the base with Renshaws chocolate brown sugarpaste textured with a nailbrush, then fit the pebbles in place.

Working with Isomalt

Ingredients

- 1kg Saracino isomalt
- Squires Kitchen Pre-cooked isomalt clear
- Saracino blue gel colour
- PME spray glaze
- Spray tin release or vegetable oil

Equipment

- Stainless steel pan
- Cotton gloves
- Thermometer
- Pyrex jug
- Silicone spatula
- Silicone moulds
- Silicone mat
- Nitrile gloves
- Blow torch
- Long flat blade knife
- Aluminium foil

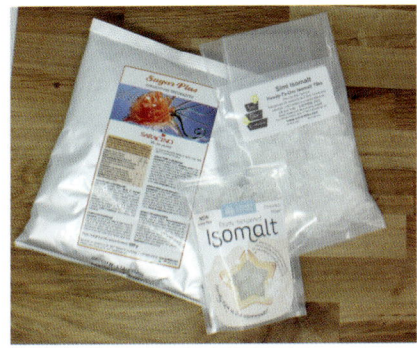

Isomalt is worked at very hot temperatures so wear long sleeves, trousers and strong shoes. Wear cotton gloves underneath strong surgical gloves. Stay safe.

You can either use pre-cooked isomalt tiles which you simply melt in the microwave following the instructions on the packet. Or you can cook your own.

It is quite a while since I have used isomalt as there wasn't much call for it when I was making wedding cakes, so on the odd occasion that I have needed it recently, I have just used the Squires Kitchen pre-cooked tiles which only need gently melting in the microwave. Perfect for small tasks.

They are very simple to use, but it is good practice to use the PME spray glaze to protect front and back to stop it getting sticky and cloudy. Especially if where you live has high humidity or is quite damp (very much describes the Welsh valleys).

After some fab refresher tuition recently from Beata Khoo, I have cooked up some Saracino isomalt and put the images below so that you can see the stages, so lets experiment with this interesting ingredient together.

(I have put Beata's details in the back for courses or just to see her fabulous work)

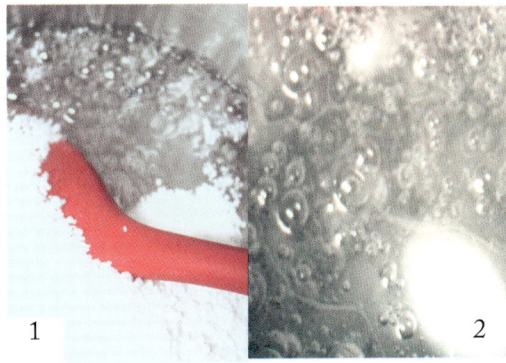
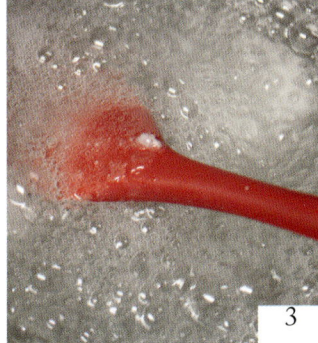
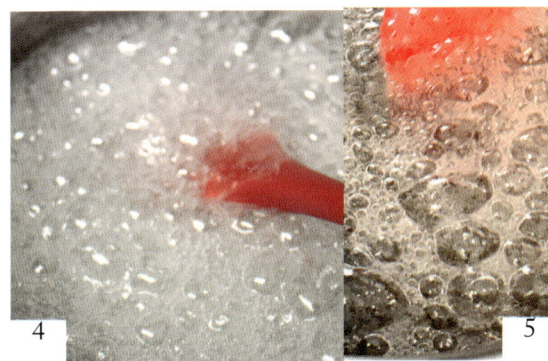

Pre-heat the hob ring the same size as the pan to full. Place 500g of isomalt into a stainless steel pan. Melt until 3/4 of the isomalt is clear then add 500g more (1). When 3/4 melted, add the final 500g and continue to heat. (2)

Use a moulded silicone spatula (without any joins as isomalt is sticky) to stir the isomalt until all of the isomalt is melted (3).

The isomalt will begin to bubble furiously (4). Watch carefully until it begins to calm down, (5) then add the thermometer. When the isomalt reaches 180C the bubbles will calm down. Plunge the pan instantly into a cold bain marie to cool.

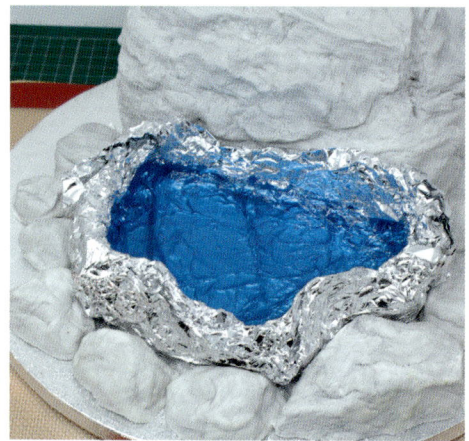

Layer 5-6 sheets of aluminium foil. Pinch up the sides and press firmly into place inside the rocks and cake to create the mould. Spray with cake release PME or smear lightly with vegetable oil, wiping

off the excess. Place re-cooked isomalt into a pyrex microwave safe jug. Melt in the microwave on medium for 20 seconds at a time until it is all melted. Slowly stir in Saracino blue gel colour with a metal

cake tester. It will bubble up a suprising amount, wait for the bubbles to burst. Pour into the greased mould, and remove the cakes and rocks until it is cold. Then peel away the foil.

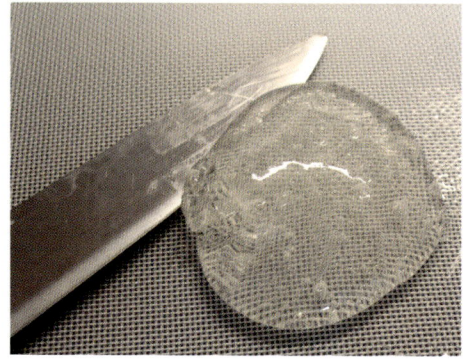

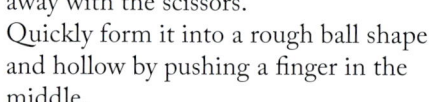

Re-heat clear isomalt in the microwave as before, allow to cool a little in a silicone container or pyrex jug. Stop the edges from cooling too much by folding them in with the knife or with a gloved finger.

Pull off a piece of the isomalt and cut it away with the scissors.
Quickly form it into a rough ball shape and hollow by pushing a finger in the middle.

Pull up sections between finger and thumb, stretching them and curling them back for the splashes. Work quickly and use a hair dryer or heat lamp to keep your work soft. A blow torch can be used too.

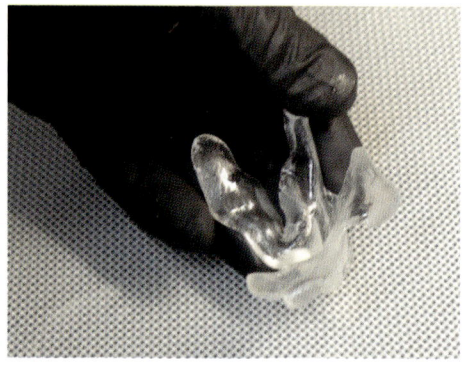

Support the finished splash and cool in front of a fan until it can support itself. Test the temperature of the isomalt as you would a baby bottle, by testing against your cheek or elbow to make sure it is cool enough to leave to rest.

Here is the finished splash (or sploosh as I like to say).
Spray all over light coats of PME spray glaze to protect from the humidity, but note that the glaze leaves a slight yellow tinge.

Isomalt is very hot, so care has to be taken when working with it. Wear cotton and nitrile gloves and long sleeves and trousers.

That said, it is loads of fun too. If you have bubbles in your work, lightly remove them with the heat of the blow torch. If a piece has gone cold, great care is needed not to crack a cold piece using a hot blow torch.

The best part is that if you make a mistake, put the isomalt in a strong food bag and smash before melting it all over again.

Melt clear pre-cooked isomalt in a pyrex jug. Cool until the isomalt is quite thick then pipe drips onto a silicone mat in a similar way as piping a drip cake. Lift up onto a tupperware container and prop into place. Put the fan on it to cool, then spray with spray glaze on both sides. Sadly , this will reduce the clarity a little.

Ice the cake board with pale grey. Airbrush black and spray with glaze. Place the prepared pond base onto the sugarpaste. Use a blow torch gently on the surface to remove any air bubbles. Too much heat will melt the isomalt and create puddles so take care.

Fix the small rocks into place on the grey sugarpaste. Use small pieces of sugarpaste to prop the rocks up to give the impression of being taller than the pond.

Roll out green sugarpaste into strips. Wrap around the board and texture with a nail brush.

Use a little clear isomalt the same consistency as when you pulled the splashes earlier. Heat the very top of the large splash gently and fix a small sausage of the clear isomalt. Heat this very carefully and press the isomalt drips into place on the cake.

Complete the design by placing small pieces of light green honey moss cake. They really do add to the cake.

Heat the base of the dragonfly wire with a blow torch and quickly push into place in one of the splashes. Paint the stem with Superwhite mixed with dipping solution if it blackens.

Mix a very small amount of grey sugarpaste let down with edible glue (melt the sugarpaste with the edible glue until it resembles chewing gum consistency, this dries very quickly).

Fix Ree Ree into place on the rock with this mixture, with one paw on the isomalt.

Add the large splashes onto the pond at the base of the rock in the same manner as adding the drips.

9

The Garden

The main garden was overgrown with beautiful flowers.

There were delicate pink roses with tiny yellow centres,

Sunflowers as tall as the sky and grass that was so very long that it was taller than him!

"There is the cow parsley!"

cried Cyril excitedly

"I'm here!"

"But wait! What was that sound?"

Purrrrrrrrr Purrrrrrrrrrr!

Cake Stand with Vegan Chocolate Biscuit Cake

My eldest son Kieran chose the delicious flavours in this chocolate biscuit cake.

One batch will also make 6 individual puddings

Ingredients

- 250g Stork biscuit block margarine (vegan)
- 500g dark chocolate (Vegan)
- 200g Bourbon biscuits
- 250g oaty Biscuits
- 5 tbsp Maple syrup
- 100g broken pecans
- 65g morello cherries
- **Cake Stand:** 500g dark Chocolate & 200g Bourbon & Oreo biscuits
- **Cake stand**: 300g dark chocolate ganache

Equipment

- 6" round cake tin or cake ring and baking tray
- Greaseproof paper
- Large mixing bowl
- 11" and 14" cake drums
- Palette knife
- Sharp knife
- Baking tray
- Spirit level

Chocolate Biscuit Cake Method

1. Melt the Stork block margarine and maple syrup carefully in the microwave in 30 second
2. increments. and stir to mix.
3. Add the chocolate chopped into 1cm pieces and stir. Microwave again in 15 second
4. increments and stir until all the lumps are gone.
5. Add the crushed biscuits, pecans and cherries and mix gently.
6. Line your cake ring using the method in chapter two (make the greaseproof 3 layers thick and 4" tall)
7. Pour in a little of the mixture and press down firmly, keep doing this until it is full and press to level then put in the fridge to set for two hours.
8. Remove from fridge and cover with cling film while still in the tin. Allow to set at room
9. temperature over night (or still in the fridge for hot climates). Remove from the tin carefully.

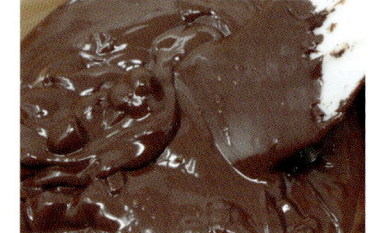

Tempering Chocolate

Temper 500g of dark chocolate by melting in the microwave first for one minute, remove from the microwave and stir to ensure that you mix the chocolate from the bottom of the bowl as it will already have melted and could otherwise burn.
(Think of baby food in the microwave, always needing to be stirred)
Continue melting the chocolate in 30 second increments until 2/3rds of the chocolate is melted as in the second picture above.

Keep stirring gently until the rest of the chocolate is melted. When ready, it should be glossy, and make a "squelch" noise when you stir away from the side of the bowl and it should leave ribbon patterns when you stir it.

Rest for 2 minutes and dip a knife to check the chocolate. It should be touchable and matte in colour in 2 minutes without leaving chocolate on your finger. (White chocolate = 5minutes and milk = 3 1/2 minutes.)

Keep your chocolate tempered by using the gentle heat of a hair dryer to keep it fluid. Or return to the microwave for 10-15 second increments,

Be careful not to overheat

To rescue it, pour half of the chocolate onto a work surface and paddle until it cools, then add back to the liquid chocolate.

Chocolate Bark

Wrap greaseproof paper around the cake and cut to 5cms longer.
Scrunch up the greaseproof and spread the tempered chocolate evenly over the greaseproof with a palette knife.

Wait approximately 1 minute to become touch dry, cover with another piece of greaseproof paper and roll up. Make a second strip to have spares and thinner strips to go around the drum edges. Chill in the fridge for 2 mins, then at room temperature for 1 hour. When you unroll the strips, the chocolate will break into pieces.

Cake Stand

Spread chocolate ganache around the sides of the chocolate biscuit cake a section at a time. Wear cotton gloves so that the chocolate does not become marked with finger prints. Break the strips to the same height as the cake for the stand, or use different heights for the cake on its own.

Score the centre of the 14" cake drum with a sharp knife, spread a little tempered chocolate onto the drum and sit the chocolate biscuit cake centrally. To check that it is still level, use a spirit level. Cover the drum with ganache. Paint the edge of the cake drum with ganache and add the chocolate bark to the edge of the cake drum using the ganache.

Remove the filling from the Bourbon and Oreo biscuits and crush the biscuits in a sandwich bag. Scatter a thin layer of the crumbled biscuits over the ganache on the cake drum.

Why not cover the top with cocoa powder and place on a display board as a fabulous cake for a celebration.

Sieve or use an icing sugar shaker to dust the surface of the cake with cocoa powder. Mark a spiral on the top with a soft tapered silicone tool.

Two Tier Cake

This design makes me dream of sunny summer days.

Sitting under the shade of a gorgeous old tree listening to the breeze rustling the leaves and the cow parsley gently swaying.

Ingredients

- Saracino 0.27mm wafer paper
- Rainbow Dust liquid colours: spring green and holly green
- Piping gel
- Biscuit earth - crumble Oreo and Bourbon biscuits and

Equipment

- Airbrush
- Glue brush
- PME scalpel
- Celpad
- PME dresden

crush in a sandwich bag.
- Squires Kitchen dust colours: eidelweiss, daffodil, vine, leaf green, violet
- Squires Kitchen cocoa butter
- Sugarflair gels: baby blue, shadow grey
- Piping gel
- 4mm matt white dragees

- 1/2" flat paint brush
- Sharp edge smoother
- Scissors
- Sugarpress paintbrushes
- Optional die cutters and die cutting machine

Bake a two tier cake in your chosen flavours. This is a 6" round by 6" tall (400g recipe) and an 8" round by 5" tall (350g recipe). Split and fill and ganache. Ice with sharp edges as in the method described in chapter two.
The 8" round needs 950g paste and the 6" round needs 850g.

Use the Sugar press to emboss the cow parsley. Use a selection of the sizes of buds and flowers. Removing and replacing as needed. Careful that you don't press in more than the single layer.

Emboss around the cow parsley with the grass, adding extra sections for more interest.
Allow to dry overnight. On hot days, I use a dehumidifier to remove moisture.

Use a half inch flat paint brush. Mix Sugarflair baby blue gel colour with Culpitt dipping solution until very runny. Paint a section of the cake.

Quickly scrunch up a sheet of kitchen paper.
Dap at the colour to blend and texture.

Repeat to cover the whole tier. Continuing to blend the colour over the tier but not to make it a solid colour.

Paint the top tier the same way. Brushing across a pattern rather than along it.
This time, leave gaps for clouds.

Mix shadow grey with dipping solution and use a small brush to add very small amounts of pale grey trailing across the clouds. We will use white cocoa butter to add highlights later.

Melt Squires Kitchen cocoa butter on a plate over a bowl half filled with boiling water. Mix eidelweiss with vine and paint inside the grass and stems.

Paint the flower sections with eidelweiss mixed with the cocoa butter.

Darken the stems with cocoa butter mixed with vine and leaf green, then add a little violet and place the join on the cow parsley stem and at the base of the flower stems.

Paint a small amount of daffodil mixed with cocoa butter into the centre of the flowers, then add a small amount of vine green dots into the very centre.

Wafer paper blossoms
Cut out the 0.27mm wafer paper shapes either using a scalpel and the templates, or use similar designs in die cutters and a die cutting machine.

Place the blossoms on a flower pad and gently press the small PME bone tool in the centre to cup the blossoms.

Paint a small amount of piping gel on the back of the flowers, and use the paintbrush handle to gently fix the large and small blossoms into place.

Here is the finished flower. You could choose to use small blossoms or all large too.

Of course you could choose just the painted blossoms instead of wafer paper.

Paint a little edible glue in the centre of the blossoms and put a 4mm matt white dragee in the centre using either tweezers or a Drageekiss.

Mix a little eidelweiss with daffodil and vine green and paint small dots on the dragees.

Blossom Die Cutter Actual Size (Use the inner line if using to cut out a template with a scissors)

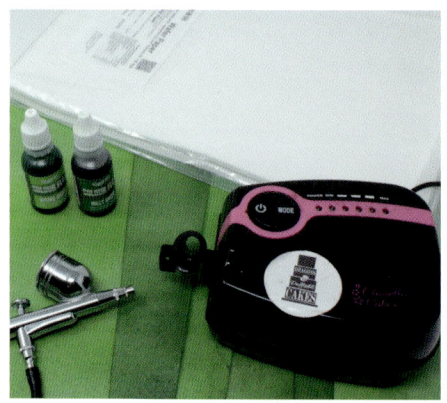

Airbrush sheets of wafer paper :
- Spring green
- Holly/ivy
- Spring green first then holly/ivy as a second layer.   Allow to dry.

Cut out wafer paper grass shapes, cutting across the shorter side of the A4 sheets. Cut each blade of grass approximately 0.5cm wide and vary the shapes slightly (cut approximately 2-3 sheets)

Place the grass on a celpad and stroke a dresden veining tool down the centre to gently crease.

Paint a thin line of piping gel down the back of the blade of grass to the height of the cake, and gently press into place on the base tier. Continue to fill the tier, with the darker grass in the background. and varying the heights of the grass. Cover the board as before.

Add as many blades of grass until you are pleased with the effect.
This tier has two sheets of A4.

Dowel the base tier by cutting the dowels equally as in chapter two. Mix sugarpaste with water to a chewing gum consistency and cover the dowel surfaces. Place the top tier centrally. Add the butterfly on the base tier.

Stencilling Cupcakes

Ingredients

- Renshaw Sugarpaste
- Coconut oil
- Squires Kitchen dusts: eidelweiss, sunflower, poppy, leaf green, Fuschia, bulrush, chestnut, hydrangea, black, bulrush, berberis
- Culpitt dipping solution

Equipment

- No.8 filbert brushes
- Sugarpress brushes
- Squires Kitchen palette knife
- Small rolling pin
- 7cm circle cutter
- The Vanilla Valley woodland animal stencil and wildflower stencil

There are lots of designs on the stencils but the technique is the same, so here are the colours.

Squirrel - Berberis, eidelweiss, chestnut, black, fuschia, bulrush

Sunflower - Chestnut, bulrush, sunflower, leaf green

Owl - Chestnut, eidelweiss, berberis, bulrush, black

Poppy - Poppy, black, leaf green

Robin - Poppy, chestnut, eidelweiss, black

Mouse - Eidelweiss, Fuschia, chestnut, bulrush, black, leaf green

Bluebell - Hydragea, leaf green

Buttercup - Sunflower, leaf green

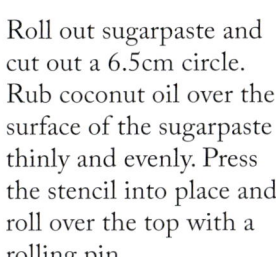

Roll out sugarpaste and cut out a 6.5cm circle. Rub coconut oil over the surface of the sugarpaste thinly and evenly. Press the stencil into place and roll over the top with a rolling pin.

The Mouse

Dust the nose, paws and tail with a mix of eidelweiss and fuschia. Dust the mouse body first with chestnut and then with a mix of chestnut and bulrush. Remove the stencil and dust the stencil gaps. Paint the eye with a sugarflair brush and black dust mixed with dipping solution.

The Poppy

Prepare the paste as before. Dust the petals and the tip of the bud with poppy dust and a little black dust in the centre. Dust the leaves, stems and base of bud with leaf green.

I have shown just two cupcakes and the background for you to see the techniques to use.

Background

Mix Hydrangea dust with dipping solution and stipple on the sky background.
Mix leaf green the same way and stipple the grass. Use a sugarpress brush and use the leaf green to paint grass stems.

Wafer Paper Sunflower

Equipment

- Glue brush
- Small sharp scissors
- Aldaval Frilly orchid petal veiner
- Aldaval all purpose leaf veiner
- Green florist tape
- Scalpel
- 18g wire, 28g wire.
- 3 pipe cleaners
- No.8 filbert brush
- Candle
- Steamer
- Plant pot

Ingredients

- Saracino 0.27mm wafer paper colour 2 sx unflower yellow and 1 with spring green and holly/ivy
- Saracino dust orange, green, brown and gel: brown
- Squires kitchen dust: sunflower, bulrush
- Squires Kitchen flowerpaste
- Piping gel
- Ground almond coloured with brown and nutkin brown
- 200g Rice krispie treats
- 2 Bourbon and 2 Oreo biscuits crushed

Airbrush two A4 sheets of Saracino wafer paper with a sunflower yellow colour (mix 5 drops of yellow with 1 drop of orange airbrush colours). Cut out at least 36 narrow petal shapes and wire them as the method described on P.34 with 28g 8cm long white wire.

Vein by holding the petal against the inverted side of the frilly orchid veiner, six inches away from the mouth of the steamer. Steam for 3 seconds, then place on the board and gently press the other half of the veiner for 10 seconds. Don't press too hard or you will split the petal.

Dust each petal with Squires Kitchen Sunflower dust, then mix a little Saracino orange in with the sunflower and dust a little at the base.

Roll a 20g wire into a 4cm wide coil smaller than the circle template. Bend the coil so that it sits flat against the wire. Grip the coil in the centre with pliers. Bend the wire down to sit under the coil

Roll a 40g pad of Squires Kitchen brown flowerpaste to the circle template. Heat the wire coil in the flame of a candle and push into the paste to fix.

Push a ball tool in the centre to hollow.
Paint the top of the centre with piping gel.
Dip into the coloured ground almond.

Sunflower Templates
This is the full calyx.
The circle below is the
size of the brown middle
with the petal template
next to it.
There are two large leaf
shapes below and an
individual calyx section.

Push the wires of the petals around the edge of the centre. Add the second row in front of the first.

Cut out the green leaves. Paint a 2cm line of glue at the base of the leaf and fix on an 8cm white 28g wire. Glue a thin wafer paper vein on top.

Vein in the steamer then dust the tips with sunflower and the rest with green.

The Calyx

Cut out two of the full calyx templates from wafer paper airbrushed with first spring green, then holly/ivy.
Cut out between 8-12 individual small calyx pieces.
Hold the wafer paper in the steam against the female side of the leaf veiner and vein each sepal and tepal of the calyx.
Hold back in the steam and use a paintbrush handle to curl back the edges.
Repeat for the individual calyx sepals and tepals.

Fitting the Calyx

Lightly glue the two whole calyx pieces in place behind the flower head first, then glue in the individual calyx sepals and tepals to fill spaces.
Tape 3 pipe cleaners around the stem and wrap in 3cm wide kitchen roll strips before taping in the leaves . Tape the stem twice and dust it with green.

To Display

Push the stem of the sunflower in the plant pot and push Rice krispie treats around it firmly.
Cover the surface with edible glue and scatter crushed Bourbon and oOeo biscuits.

Look who made the pawprints.

Say hello to Luna.

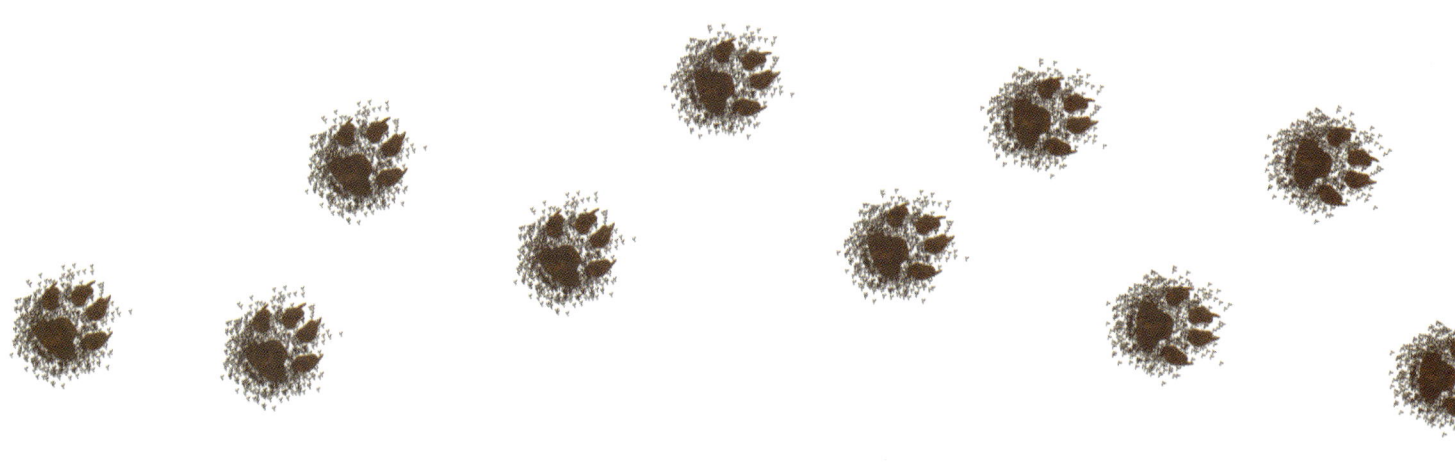

Miaaaaaoooooow

10
Luna the Cat

Luna the cat was sleeping on the front doorstep,
curled up tightly waiting for Mr Morris to finish gardening.

"I can do this! I CAN do this!"
said Cyril to himself and bravely stepped forward.

Luna opened one eye and stretched lazily.

"Hello there, you must be Cyril" said Luna

"You know me?" said Cyril

"But of course!" said Luna, "I have been waiting for you"

Mr Morris walked towards Cyril and Luna and said,
"There you are!
After such a big adventure, you must be very hungry"

and he turned and pointed to a blanket on the grass filled with
lots of delicious food.

"Why there are my friends!" said Cyril.
He could see Olly, Mr Bird, Sammy, Squeak, Dewi, Ree Ree, Mervyn
and even Rusty the fox who gave him a little wave.

Not so scary after all.

But what happens next?

Make sure you turn to P.123 for the end of the
story.

Luna the Cat

Rich Chocolate Cake

Ingredients

- 500g tub stork
- 250g block stork
- 200g plain chocolate.
- 525g soft light brown sugar.
- 600g self raising flour
- 100g cocoa powder
- 12 eggs 670g beaten
- 180g golden syrup
- 1 1/2 tsp vanilla extract
- 1 level tsp baking powder
- 1 tsp coffee dissolved in 2 tbsp milk

This cake is a delicious and moist cake for both wedding or sculpted cakes, but is best frozen after you have split and filled and before you carve or ganache.

Method

1. Pre-heat the oven to 170C/ Gas 3.
2. Grease and line a 2 10" square baking tin (3-4" tall) and an 8" square tin placing a metal piping nail with the nail point upright by placing on the greased tin and placing the greaseproof paper on top. This will help conduct the heat to ensure the cake is cooked through.
3. Chop chocolate up into 1cm pieces. Place in a bowl with the butter and melt either in the microwave or over hot water.
4. Place the margarine into a mixer and beat until soft.
5. Sieve the flour, cocoa powder and baking powder.
6. Add the sifted flour and then the sifted cocoa powder.
7. Put all other ingredients into the mixer and mix on low, adding the flour gradually.
8. Share the mix out into the three tins so that they are the same height.
9. Bake for 35-40 minutes or until the skewer comes out clear.
10. Cool in the tins on a cooling rack. Allow to mature overnight before use.

Equipment

- 2 x 10" square lined cake tin
- 1 x 8" square lined cake tin

Luna template here and on p.119 are for carving the cake. Trace and line up using front right paw. The ganache and sugarpaste will increase the size by 1cm each direction.

Sculpted Cat Cake with Edible Supports

Ingredients

- 10" square chocolate cake
- Buttercream
- 900g dark chocolate ganache
- Sugarpaste
- Squires Kitchen dust colours: berberis, chestnut, bulrush, black and pink.
- Black Saracino pasta model
- SK white flowerpaste
- Unbreakable gel
- Culpitt dipping solution
- PME Spray Glaze
- Shell and Shine
- 100g Callebaut 811 dark chocolate callets
- 60g rice krispie treats

Equipment

- Serrated knife
- Scalpel
- PME dresden
- Airbrush
- Dusting brushes
- Detail
- Brushes
- Palette
- FMM Bone tool
- PME Scribe
- Greaseproof paper
- Nailbrush
- Pen lid
- 14" cake drum
- Ribbon and double sided tape
- 14" square cake card.

It is always easier to freeze a cake before carving. Split and fill your cake, then cover with cling film and freeze for a couple of hours. Carve while frozen, returning to the freezer for half an hour before you coat with ganache.

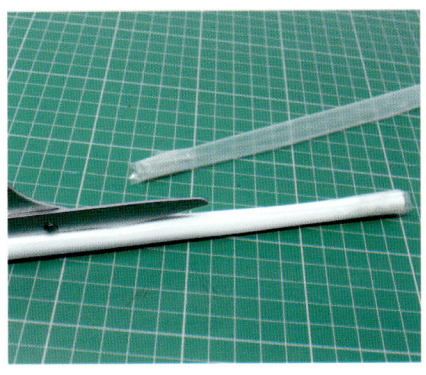

Edible leg Supports

Temper 100g of dark chocolate following the instructions in chapter 9. Half fill a piping bag with the chocolate and use an elastic band or clip to seal the bag.

Cut FMM cake straws lengthwise with scissors. Seal one end with cellotape. Put the point of the piping bag in the straw and pipe so that the straw slightly over-flows. Set in the fridge for 20 minutes. Open the straw and remove the chocolate stick.

Trace the template onto greaseproof and cut out. Place the template on the 14" sq cake card and cut around it with strong kitchen scissors. (Only have a 10" square? Add a section for the lower leg and tail and glue gun onto the main card. File the edges of the cake card.)

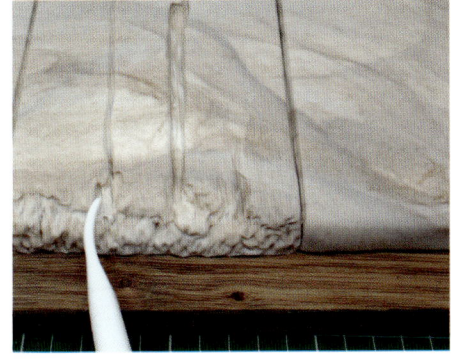

The Cake Board

Dampen the cake board with cooled boiled water. Roll out 950g white sugarpaste marbled with dark brown paste colour and cover the board. Press the metal royal icing rule firmly into the sugarpaste

to create the gaps between the planks for the decking.
Use the Cerart 305 to mark the woodgrain. Pushing in the tool to shape the ends of the split wood.

Add more detail with the Cerart hard point. Use the tool to add wood worm holes and to drag splits. Push your thumb into the board and pinch the top and bottom to a point, then add splits above and below the knot.

Repeat the texture on the far side, then add lines on the two other sides.
Indent the nail holes using the handle of the Cerart hard point tool.

Dust gaps and grooves of the board with Squires Kitchen bulrush and black. Dust the board with a mixture of chestnut and bulrush dust colours. Airbrush bulrush to add depth and allow to dry.

Wipe the board gently from inside to where we have split the wood with damp kitchen paper.
Spray with a couple of coats of PME spray glaze for a matt finish, or shell and shine for a shiny surface.

Carving the Cake

Cut the cake card to the template. Spread chocolate buttercream and place the cake on top. Carve the outline with the serrated knife. Reserve the trimmings.

Use a scalpel to cut the lines into the greaseproof template.
Place the template on the cake and cut through the lines in the template to mark shallow lines.

Carve the belly area lower than the head by removing a slice.
Spread buttercream onto the cats leg and tail and using the template, cut out from the spare offcuts and fix onto the cake card.

Here is the front half of the cat carved. Leave the back thigh taller. Add offcuts to build it up if neccessary (I reserved the offcuts for the chocolate pot later in the chapter)

Round off the head shape, carving the chin to a point, emphasising the muzzle shape and carve the cheeks

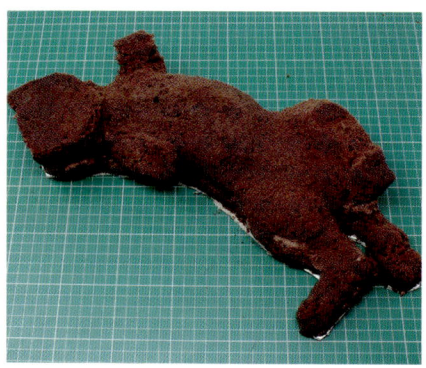

Curve the belly area by sculpting with the serrated knife.

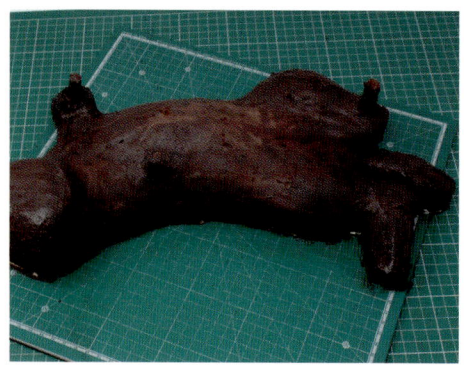

Cover the cake with dark chocolate ganache. Applying either with a cranked palette knife, or with a piece of flexi smoother. Push choc sticks into the legs. Allow to set at room temperature until ganache is quite firm. This will take longer in warmer weather.

Melt 200g of marshmallows in the microwave until it rises and is fluffy. Stir in 200g of rice krispies. Leave at room temperature for 30 minutes until you can touch it without it sticking to your finger.

Shape each paw from 20g of rice krispie treats.
Carefully squeezing it firmly into place around the chocolate sticks.
Quickly wrap with cling film and leave overnight to set before removing the cling film and covering with ganache.

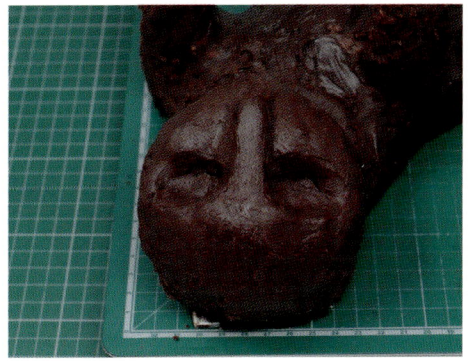

Use 200g of the remaining ganache and add a long nose onto the cat, a forehead and cheeks. Smooth over the ganache with your fingers. The heat of your hands will warm and blend it together.

Knead 1.2kg of Renshaw white sugarpaste and roll out longer and wider than the cat (not including the paws). Warm the ganache and lay the sugarpaste over the cake. Smooth into place. Use scissors to cut into sections around the paws if required, but blend the joins straight away. Cover with cling film.

Eyes

Make eyes from 6.5g of flowerpaste each. Paint on the eye sunflower yellow iris, add leaf green and chestnut around the outside and a line of black around that. Paint the pupil black and add hightlights in eidelweiss. Spray with Shell and shine before fitting into place.

Add the eyelids in white Renshaw extra by adding the 1.6g lower eyelid first then the 3g upper eyelid. Blend them onto the face and leave extra for the socket around the eye.

Add the muzzle from 7.5g of paste and the mark the side of the nose & centre of the muzzle with the PME dresden and the nostrils with a 2mm ball tool

Mark in the mouth area with the PME veining tool curving around the muzzle. Scratch the face texture following the direction of the fur starting at the nose with the scalpel and

using the PME veining tool as you move away. Lifting the handle of the PME veining tool higher means you lift the paste higher and get more texture.

Emphasise the fur on the cheeks by slicing into the fur with a mixture of the scalpel and the PME veining tool. Indent the whisker holes with a scribe tool.

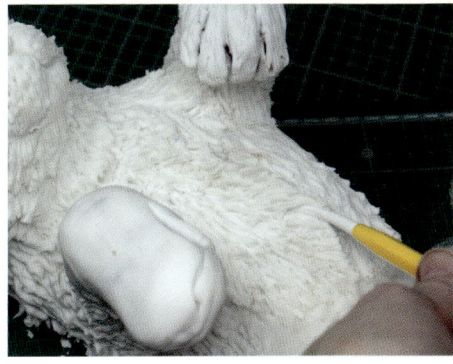

Continue to texture down onto the chest, marking the raised section of fur down the middle. Follow the shape of the body.

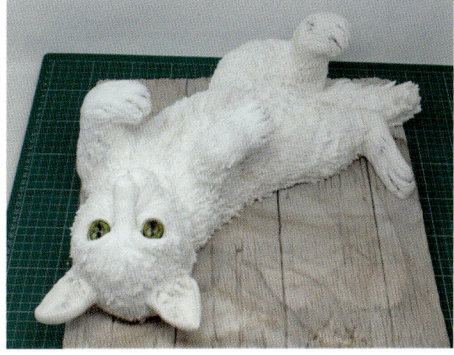

Continue texturing the cake. Take care when texturing the paws, supporting them as you work. Add deeper texture on the upper paws with the PME veining tool and use the scalpel on the ends of the paws.

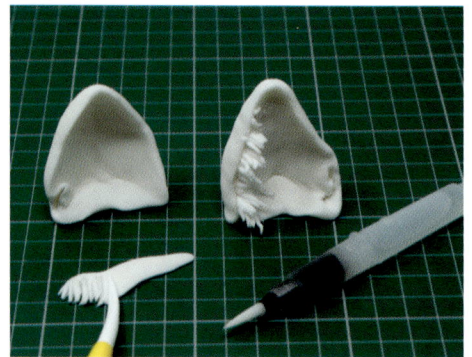

Shape the ears out of 45g 50:50 SFP and sugarpaste into a 7cm tall triangle. Use the scalpel to mark the texture on the back of the ears, and add sliced strips of paste for extra fur inside the ears. Fix into place and use the veining tool to blend.

Fix the cat shaped cake card into place on the decking board using tempered chocolate.

Roll black claws and three sets of black pads for the feet as above, and one pink set. Glue the pads into place.
Fix the claws by pushing the veining tool in first, glue and push them into the hole.

Colour

Begin dusting the colour onto luna. I used Saracino black and a large brush. Stippling the colour on.
Don't worry about the eyes as we glazed them and can clean them again.

Meow

Add Culpitt dipping solution to the colour palette and use the Sugarpress fine brushes to pick out dark areas and individual hairs.
Emphasise the upper eyelids.

Finish Luna by adding unbreakable gel whiskers made in the same method as the spiders web in chapter three. These had Sugarflair superwhite dust added to the mix. Paint the occasional whisker and the eyebrow whiskers white.

Vegan Granola Bars

My son Matthew makes his own granola and has shared his favourite recipe with us. Shaping these with cookie cutters and drizzling with dark chocolate makes a delicious alternative to cake.

Choose whichever dried fruit and nuts you please to create your favourite taste.

The image left shows the baked Granola and the additional ingredients required to transform it into bars.

Ingredients

- 3 cups rolled oats
- 1 1/2 cups mixed nuts incl almonds, cashews, hazelnuts
- 1 cup mixed seeds - whole flax, pumpkin, sunflower
- 1 cup mixed dried fruit - dates, cranberries, apricots, light golden raisins
- 1/2 tsp salt
- 1/2 tsp nutmeg
- 1/2 tsp ginger
- 1 tsp cinnamon
- 1/2 cup veg oil
- 1/3 cup agave nectar

Equipment

- Cookies from chapter 1 plus other shapes such as heart, circle, hexagon
- Baking Tray
- Greaseproof paper

Bars

- 1/4 cup maple syrup
- 2/3 cup peanut butter
- 4 cups granola mix
- 1/4 tsp vanilla extract
- PME release spray or veg oil
- Sea salt

This is such a pretty granola mixture

Store in a tupperware container in the fridge for a week.....

.......if it lasts that long.

Granola Method

1. Pre-heat the oven to 180C gas 4.
2. Chop the nuts and fruit small
3. Mix all the dry ingredients together.
4. Whisk the wet mix in a separate bowl.
5. Pour the wet mix slowly into the dry mix.
6. Line a baking tin with a sheet of greaseproof paper which also covers the sides. Bake for 20 minutes or until no longer wet, and slightly golden. It should be still moist but not crispy. Stir halfway through.

Granola Bars Method

1. To turn into granola bars, heat the maple syrup and peanut butter together
2. Add to 2 cups of the mixture along with a pinch of sea salt and a 1/4 tsp vanilla extract.
3. Spray cookie cutters with PME spray release, place on greaseproof and fill with the mix. Leave to set.
4. Temper dark chocolate following the instructions in chapter 9. Half fill a piping bag with the chocolate and drizzle over the bars to finish.

Mervyn the Mole Pudding

Ingredients

- Chocolate biscuit cake pudding
- Oreo & Bourbon crumbs
- Rich tea biscuits
- 25g Saracino pasta model skintone
- Dessicated coconut
- Green gel colours
- Saracino dusts: skintone, pink, brown, black, violet
- A small amount of Ganache
- Bourbon filling

Equipment

- PME Scalpel
- Sugarpress brushes
- Cerart Hard point
- 1mm dotting tool
- PME Scalpel
- PME Bone tool
- PME Dresden
- Silicone brush
- Pudding moulds
- Glue Brush

Make the chocolate pudding by polishing the inside of an individual pudding container with a soft clean piece of cotton and filling with the chocolate biscuit recipe from chapter 9 (makes 6). Refrigerate for two hours until the pudding releases from the mould.

Spread ganache on the top of the pudding.

Knead the filling from the Bourbon biscuits into a paste. Roll into a ball and place on top of the pudding.
Push a thumb into the centre.

Press chocolate biscuit crumbs onto the top and sides.

Chocolate biscuit crumbs were made in Chapter 9 from crushed Oreo and Bourbon biscuits.

Add more ganache to the base of the pudding. Crush rich tea biscuits in a bag and add a little dessicated coconut. Colour with green gel colour mixed with a little water or alchohol and add to the bag. Press the green crumbs around the base of the pudding.

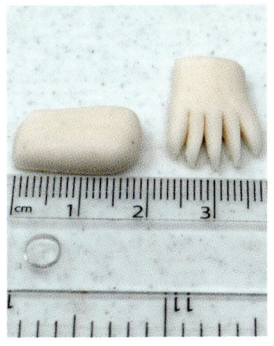

Paws

Cut 2.5g of saracino skintone in half and shape as above. Cut wedges out with a scalpel to separate the fingers.

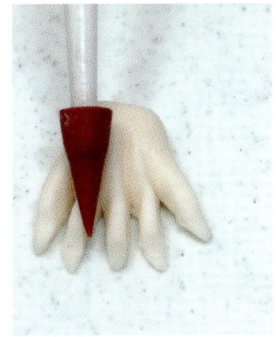

Mark between fingers with the hard point by stroking the point of the tool backwards and leaning against the back of the paw.

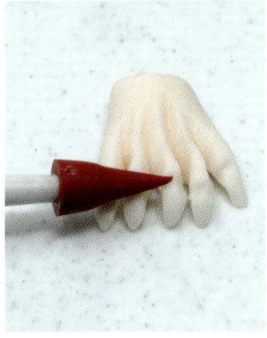

Press the point of the tool to mark the cuticle of the claws. Pinch the claws to a point.

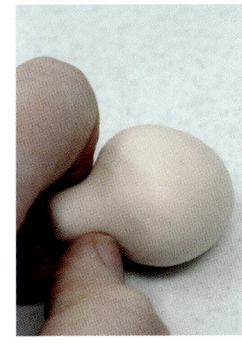

Head

Roll 22g of skintone into a ball. Pinch and pull the muzzle area.

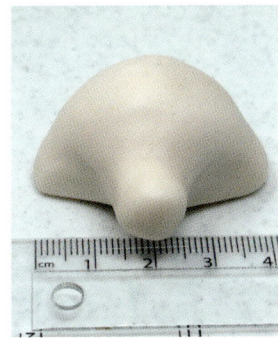

Stroke down the sides of the head to widen and shape it as the image above.

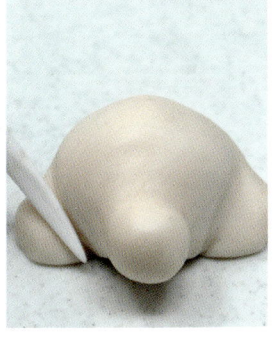

Use the veining tool to separate the head from the shoulder area by stroking from the base and up to the top of the shoulder.

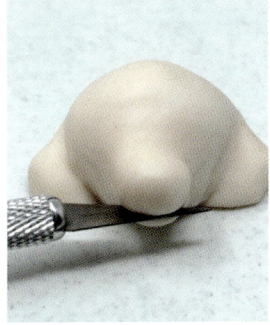

Push the scalpel horizontally into the muzzle to open the mouth. Neaten the ends by pushing the point of the scalpel in.

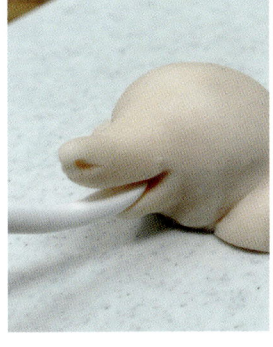

Push the PME Dresden into the mouth to both cup the chin and hollow the mouth. Push the Hard point tool into the nostrils.

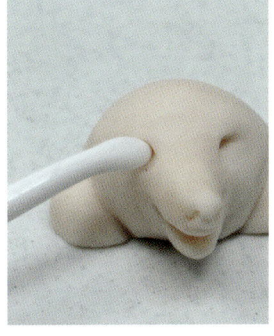

Push the Dresden upside down to shape the eye socket. Stroke it with your finger or a PME bone tool to soften the shape.

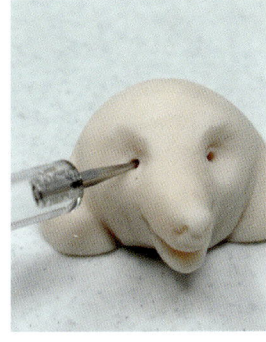

Push the 1mm ball dotting tool in to create the hole for the eye socket.

Scratch the fur for the mole using a scalpel. Scratch using the nose as the centre of the clock, and all the fur radiates towards the number.

Colouring

Dust the nose first with a little Saracino pink, and then add a little violet to add depth. Dust inside the mouth.

Dust the mole with black dust, avoiding the eye and muzzle area. The overdust will add enough colour. Gently dust inside the mouth.

Roll a tiny sausage of black saracino and cut two tiny pieces. Roll and glue in the eye. Paint the eye with glaze or edible glue to add shine.

Glue the paws onto the side of the shoulders, and fix the mole into the pudding with a little ganache.

Pastillage Plate

Ingredients

- 1 Egg white
- 250g Icing sugar
- 1 tsp Gum Tragacanth
- Airbrush colours: Rainbow dust airbrush colour

- dark green
- Cornflour
- SK holly/ivy gel
- corn flour puff
- Spectrum flow shell and shine

Equipment

- 20cm Side plate
- Icing sugar shaker

- Scalpel
- Rolling pin

Pastillage Method

1. Beat the eggs and pour into the mixer.
2. Add icing sugar a little at a time until the first batch is incorporated.
3. Sprinkle the gum tragacanth over the bowl and cover with a tea towel.
4. Leave for ten minutes and then turn out onto the remaining sieved icing sugar.
5. Knead quickly incorporating as much of the icing sugar as is needed to achieve a firm paste consistency.
6. Knead until the paste grows whiter.

Store in two layers of food bags in a tupperware container in the fridge or freezer, but it is always best used from fresh.

**Pastillage is a really useful building block paste.
It can be used for edible place settings and for constructing buildings.
The plate will take 2-3 days to be completely dry. It will dry faster if you
have identical plates. After 24 hours, dust the back of the second plate
with cornflour, and gently place on top of the first plate and flip over.
Remove the original plate to allow the back to dry.**

Colour the paste with SK holly/ivy. Roll out on icing sugar to 2-3mm thick. Dust your plate with cornflour and place the pastillage on top. Quickly push down into the plate to take the shape, especially for the centre indentation. Trim the edges with a scalpel and smooth the edge with your finger.

Airbrush the outer edge of the plate with Sugarflair dark green. Allow to dry.

Spray two coats with shell and shine allowing to dry between coats and fully dry before placing dessserts carefully on it.
Store in a dry place in a cardboard box with either rice, salt, or silica gel nearby to absorb moisture.

Carefully place the mole pudding on the centre of the plate where there is the most support.

Next place the vegetable cupcake

Finally, stand up the Cyril the squirrel granola bar drizzled with delicious dark chocolate.

The Celebration

"WELL DONE CYRIL!"
they all shouted excitedly, clapping their paws and flapping their wings at him.

"HAPPY BIRTHDAY!!!!"
"Happy Birthday?" said Cyril "My birthday?"
and he looked very puzzled.

"hoo-hoo-hoo-hoo" laughed Olly the Owl,
"You lost count! Today is your ninth moon,
you really are all grown-up after all."
And everyone cheered.

Olly wrapped a huge soft wing around Cyril and gave
him a gentle squeeze.
"Well done Cyril, we are so proud of you"

"Thank you Olly" said Cyril shyly and reached to grab a
chocolate pot topped with little acorns.
Just as he was about to take a bite he said

"That was quite an adventure"

"Oh! That was nothing" said Luna
"Wait until you see what we found!"

..............But that is a story for another time

(To say thank you for reading, turn over for a sneak peek at the next story.)

Excerpt from Book 2
"The lands of Faerie"

Cyril crept cautiously around the living room Door. "What could it be?" he wondered.

Mr Morris said there was a special guest in his house. Then he saw it...........him.......
He was a beatiful Corgi puppy.

"Oh hello!" cried Cyril in delight. "So nice to meet you, I'm sure we will be great friends".

"Oh don't get too attached," said Luna, "he is promised to the Faeries."

"What!!" said Cyril, "OH NO!"

"Oh it's okay" promised Luna, "It's a great honour, for he is to be a Faerie steed to the Prince himself."

"How wonderful!" said Cyril, then he looked down sadly.   "I wish I could go with him."

"What a great idea" said Luna, "You should take him to the Faerie lands over the stream."

"Oh can I?" said Cyril, "I promise I will take him there safely, but how will I know the way?"

"I can help you there" said Olly with a smile. "Here is a map I drew last time I went" and he handed Cyril a map drawn on leaves that had been carefully sewn together with grass.

"Why so many leaves?" wondered Cyril, curiously touching the delicate map.

"Well Faerie is really big Cyril," said Olly, "It is a magical world after all, so each time it needs more space, it simply grows.   But you can't tell how big it is from the skies because the magic fools you.   So each time I discovered more, I added more leaves.
But don't lose it, it is the only copy."

"I will be very careful" said Cyril. Carefully folding the precious map.

"Here" said Mr Morris. "This will help you keep it safe" and he handed Cyril a beautiful bag with a long strap. Cyril slipped it over his head and patted it safely into place.

"So.....are you ready?" said Luna "You should leave now before it gets dark. Here are enough supplies to get you there."

"Oh thank you very much" said Cyril, his eyes shining brightly with excitement.

...................but to find out what happens next you will have to wait.
To be Continued in ....

"The lands of Faerie"

Grateful Thanks

A book cannot be written without the support of a great many people, so please bear with me here.

First, to my family. My wonderful husband Adrian and my incredible boys Kieran and Matthew.
Thank you for always listening as I ran all my ideas past you...................repeatedly! I can't thank you enough. Sorry for all the microwave meals and chaotic house and all the spell checking.
Thank you for the recipes boys, they are absolutely delicious.

Thank you to the talented Emma of Emelizabeth Illustration. I was honoured to be able to commision the gorgeous illustrations of Cyril.

To my wonderful supportive Mam Laura and Step Dad Glan, My Sister Beth and her husband Grant and daughter Lola. You have all constantly been there supporting me even when I caked you out, which was often.

Thanks must also go to my Uncle Glen, Aunty Kim, Emma, Mark and their families, for constantly being my guinea pigs. To our beloved Leigh-Andrew, may he forever soar amongst the stars, sorely missed along with our wonderful Nanny and Grampy - the inspiration for Mr Morris.

My Cake journey has lasted 23 years so far, and I have been given so many wonderful opportunities along the way.

I am hesitant to list names here for fear of missing anybody out, but if I do, I apologise profusely, you know who you are.

Particular thanks have to go to Beverley and Robert Dutton for the honour of writing for Squires Kitchen, for exhibiting and teaching at the Exhibition and travelling to China to represent you there. I constantly pinch myself for being that fortunate. I treasure the times at the Squires Kitchen exhibition, it was a home away from home with wonderful people that were so generous sharing their knowledge and expertise. I made so many good friends over the years. CMSHO are a constant support.

To all the wonderful artists that I have had the honour to be inspired by and learn from along the way, especialy Tombi Peck, Alan Dunn, Sir Eddie Spence MBE, Lindy Smith and Janet Side. Your books, demonstrations and classes are a constant inspiration to me.

Thanks to Julie Askew and Leeanne Cooper for the opportunity to write for Cake Decoration and Sugarcraft Magazine.
Thank you Rosie Mazumder for giving me the honour of being named one of the Top 10 UK Cake Artists of the year 2018. That meant such a lot to me.

Thank you Rose Dummer, Suzi Witt, Paul Bradford and David Brice, such an honour to film with you all.

Thanks to everyone that has asked me to take part in their projects and
all the collaborations - Go Team Welsh Cakes - Cara, Paul and Rob.

My wonderful weekly students, you are my anchor. I wouldn't have achieved any of this without you. To all the students in day classes I have taught and to all the British Sugarcraft Guild branches and sugarcraft clubs that have hosted me, such wonderful friends all over, it is truly always a pleasure.

Thanks to Natalie Porter for the invaluable advice, you are an absolute treasure.

Last but not least, to Melanie Underwood.
I just can't thank you enough not just for the incredible opportunities you have given me at Cake International, but for the constant words of encouragement, I don't think I would have written this book without your belief in me.

I am privileged to be able to spend my working life creating in cake, but when you also get the opportunity to create with friends, it becomes magical and for that I will always be grateful.

The beatiful collection of illustrations that Emma created for the book.

With Grateful Thanks to

Renshaw is the leading British manufacturer of Sugarpaste, Marzipan, Frostings, Caramels and Mallows. Renshaw supply retailers, specialist sugar craft shops, bakeries, wholesalers, and manufacturers. In addition their products are exported worldwide. Renshaw have been manufacturing cake decorating ingredients since 1898, and have held a Royal Warrant since 1950. With their long history of manufacturing quality cake ingredients Renshaw have seen many changing trends and techniques in cakes over the decades. However, one thing that does not change is the great passion Renshaw users have for creating inspirational works of art using the wide range of quality Renshaw products.
For more information visit : **www.renshawbaking.com**

The Vanilla Valley is one of the UK's leading names in cake decorating supplies and equipment.
Our aim is to provide all of the leading brands and popular cake making products to both professionals and home bakers.
www.thevanillavalley.co.uk
sales@thevanillavalley.co.uk

For over 30 years, Squires Kitchen has been supplying high-quality cake decorating and sugarcraft products to cake makers all over the world. Focused on design and innovation, they manufacture over 2,000 products, including the UK's market-leading flowerpaste, Sugar Florist Paste (SFP), and SK Fairtrade Sugarpaste, the professionals' choice for flawless cake covering and the first sugarpaste in the UK to be Fairtrade-certified.
Call 0330 223 4466 or visit
www.squires-shop.com

"We Love Pastry" is our strapline, showing our love and passion for the world of confectionery. The steady growth of Saracino in Europe and in other major World markets is proof that we love what we do and never stop looking for the best quality. Visit our Website for the full range of products. Happy Cake Designing!
Saracino Srl, Via Retrone 34, 36077, Altavilla Vicentina VI, Italy. info@saracinodolci.co.uk
www.saracinodolci.co.uk

Crafty Designs are an irish owned family business based in Meath. Sugar Press fondant letter stamps & boards.
www.craftydesigns.ie

FPC Sugarcraft is a family run business producing a wide range of food contact grade silicone moulds, suitable for use by home bakers and professionals alike.
All of our products are made by hand, with care, in the UK, using the highest quality materials for precise, repeatable results.
www.fpcsugarcraft.co.uk

Clairella Cakes Airbrush & bespoke products by multi award winning cake artist & tutor Claire Anderson, who is internationally renowned for her airbrushing style. Her products are available worldwide from amazon. For more information please visit
www.Clairellacakes.com.

Beata Khoo. Award-winning cake designer specialising in Isomalt decorations and sculptures. I teach in and outside of the UK, I also have online training videos.
My Sweet Passion Cakes, Brighton and Hove, UK
Tel: 0740 3454313
www.mysweetpassion.com

Photographs: By Rhianydd Webb. Mad Hatter Wedding Cake photograph on P.128 by Allistair Thorpe.
Cyril cake design inspired by a wildlife photograph by Andre Villeneuve.

ISBN 978-1-9162428-0-7

About the Author

Rhianydd is a proud Mam to Kieran 24 and Matthew 21 and lives in her home town of Pontypridd, South Wales with her husband Adrian and her family close by.

A great lover of music, Rhianydd completed a music degree in Bath. She enjoys arts and crafts, so cake decorating, initially a hobby, became a wonderful way to be a stay at home Mam.

Rhianydd set up Dragons and Daffodils Cakes in 1999, creating all manner of celebration, corporate and around 3000 wedding cakes. Initially from home, and later alongside wonderful staff in her premises in South Wales. She has created three solo features for Cake International with the kind permissions of the Enid Blyton Society, and Toni Di'Terlizzi.

Rhianydd is an accredited demonstrator for the British Sugarcraft Guild and teaches weekly classes in South Wales for which she won the NIACE award. She travels to teach, and has taught all over the UK including at the prestigeous Renshaw Academy, Squires Kitchen Exhibitions and Cake International. She recently travelled abroad for the first time to teach and judge in Shanghai on behalf of Squires Kitchen.

For the last twenty years, Rhianydd has written tutorials for magazines including Squires Kitchen Cakes & Sugarcraft and Wedding Cakes: A design Source; Cake Decoration and Sugarcraft Magazine; Cake International Magazine; Cake Masters Magazine; the British Sugarcraft Guild Newsletter and ICES Newsletter.

In 2014, Rhianydd began competing at Cake International, and after achieving a number of gold medals in her favourite categories of Wedding cakes, sugar flowers, small decorative and decorative exhibit, including 1st , 2nd and 3rd place she was proud to join the judging team in 2017.
She also holds gold medals in wedding cakes and small decorative and 1st place in miniatures at Salon Culinaire.

In 2018 she was named one of the UK Top 10 Cake Artists by Cake Masters Magazine.

128